BREAKING EVIL YOKES

BREAKING BLOODLINE CURSES &
REEDEMING YOUR BLOODLINE

PRAYER M. MADUEKE

ISBN: 978-1545144213

Published by Prayer Publications.

Printed in the United States of America.

4 Free Ebooks

In order to say a 'Thank You' for purchasing *Breaking Evil Yokes*, I offer these books to you in appreciation. Click or type **madueke.com/free-gift** in your browser.

Message from the Author

I want to see you succeed, grow, and break free from negativity and obstacles. My hope is for you to thrive, unaffected by negative influences and challenging situations. Because of that, please permit me to introduce two courses that I believe passionately will help you:

1. To break the evil altars and powers of your father's house, The role of altars in the realm of existence is very key because altars are meeting places between the physical and the spiritual, between the visible and the invisible.

    Unless a man cuts off the evil flow from the power of his father's house, he will not fulfil his destiny. <u>Click here</u> to learn more about <u>my course</u> on how to tear down unholy altars and close the enemy's entryways into your life!

2. To help you seamlessly break iron-like problems, illness, delayed marriage, poverty, or any long-standing battle.

    Discover <u>the transformative power of Christian fasting and prayer</u>. Remember, Matthew 17:21 teaches us, *"But this kind of demon does not go out except by prayer and fasting."* Ready to overcome your struggles? <u>Click here</u> to learn more about this course.

Embrace the journey ahead with faith, for through prayer, fasting, and the dismantling of evil altars, you shall unlock the doors to spiritual liberation and divine breakthrough. May your path be illuminated by His grace as you walk towards a life free from bondage.

If you're seeing this from the physical copy, type the link: <u>madueke.com/courses</u> in your browser to view all the courses on my website.

Prayer Madueke
CHRISTIAN AUTHOR

Christian Counselling

We were created for a greater purpose than only survival and God wants us to live a full life.

If you need prayer or counselling, or if you have any other inquiries, please visit the counselling page on my website to know when I will be available for a phone call.

Click or type **links.madueke.com/counselling** in your browser.

Let's Connect on Youtube ▶

Join me on my YouTube channel, "Prayer M. Madueke," where I share powerful insights, guidance, and prayers for spiritual breakthroughs.

Subscribe today to unlock the secrets of the Kingdom and embrace an abundant life. Let's grow together!

Click or type **links.madueke.com/youtube** in your browser.

TABLE OF CONTENTS

1. What Is A Yoke?...13

    • Examples Of Biblical Yokes 16

    • What Of The Iron Gate? 31

2. Different Kinds Of Yoke 39

    • Yoke Of The Neck 39

    • Yoke Of Iron.................................47

    • The Yoke Of Oxen.................................55

    • Grievous Or Heavy Yoke 71

3. The Yoke Of Transgression 76

4. The Yoke Of The Youth 116

5. The Yoke Of The Jaw.................................132

    • Jaw Yoke Upon The Dumb 134

    • Who Was John The Baptist?.................................149

    • What Did God Do With The Spirit Of Elijah? 151

6. Yoke Of Bondage 159

    • What Is Bondage? 162

    • The Yoke Of Unbelief.................................163

7. The Yoke Of Wood 188

8. Believer's Yokes Broken By God 197

- How To Break Your Evil Yokes By Faith And By Prayers 210

- By Understanding How To Praise God 215

- Removal Of Every Idol................................... 220

- Encounter With The Only True Yoke 223

9. Prayer Warfare Section 230

- 271 Enough Is Enough Prayers........................ 231

- Let My Pharaoh Die 262

- Let My Destiny Escape By Fire........................ 265

- I Refuse To Be Dominated................................. 268

- My Eagle Must Fly 271

- O Lord, Take Away My Burden 276

- Eaters Of Flesh And Drinkers Of Blood 279

- Prayers To Break Yoke Of Disfavor 282

- Prayers To Break The Yoke Of Ministerial Failure 287

- Prayers To Break Yoke Of Sexual Immorality 294

- Prayers To Break The Yoke Of Marital Break Up 299

- Prayers To Break The Yoke Of Drunkenness.305

- Prayers To Break Yoke Of Iniquity 310

- Prayers To Break Yoke Of Bad Habits 315

- Prayers To Break Yoke Of Witchcraft 320

- Prayers To Break Yoke Of Evil Inheritance.....326

- Prayers To Break Yoke Of Rising And Falling 331

- Prayers To Break Yoke Of Environmental Forces 335

- Prayers To Break Yoke Of Sleeplessness 340

- Prayers To Break Yoke Of Infirmities..............345

- Prayers To Break Yoke Of Hardship 350

- Prayers To Break Yoke Of Almost There 354

- Prayers To Break Yoke Of Curses...................358

- Prayers To Break Yoke Of Rejection 363

- Prayers To Break Yoke Of Limitation..............368

- Prayers To Break Yoke Of Loneliness 372

- Prayers To Break Yoke Of Weakness..............376

- Prayers To Break Yoke Of Satan 379

- Prayers To Break Yoke Of Evil Pattern 383

- Prayers To Break Yoke Of Back To Square One 387

- Prayers To Break Yoke Of Fear 390

- Prayers To Break Yoke Of Spiritual Marriage. 394

- Prayers To Break Yoke Of Placenta Bondage. 398

- Prayers To Break Yoke Of Water Spirits 402

- Prayers To Break Yoke Of Powerlessness 406

- Prayers To Break Yoke Of Setback 409

- Prayers To Break Yoke Of Recurring Problems 413

- Prayers To Break Yoke Of Unforgivingness 416

- Prayers To Break Evil Appetite 419

- Prayers To Break Yoke Of Impossibility 422

- Bibliography .... **Error! Bookmark not defined.**

CHAPTER 1

WHAT IS A YOKE?

Literally, a yoke is a wooden bar or frame tied to the heads or necks two animals to work together. The yoke significantly makes it impossible for each of the animals to operate freely or independently.

However, for humans, a yoke would be -

- An arched device formerly laid on the neck of a defeated person.

- A frame fitted to a person is shoulder to carry a load in two equal portions.

- A bar by which the end of the tongue of a wagon or carriage *is* suspended from the collars of the harness.

- A crosspiece on the· head of a boat's rudder.

- The control device for an airplane's ailerons that is mounted on a column, which also serves to operate the elevator.

- A frame from which a bell hung.

- A clamp or similar piece that embraces two parts to hold or unite them in position.

Two animals or more can he yoked together for easy control. Yoke IS an oppressive agency; Yokes are made to bring a person under servitude or bondage. It is an oppressive agency to link up a person to problems. A Christian who *is* married to an unbeliever is under a yoke. There are many kinds of yokes. We have personal yoke, family yoke, tribal yoke, environmental yoke, a native or gullible inhabitant of a rural area or small town. Some yokes are common in some area or with people.

To be under a yoke *is* like carrying a burden or load. A worrisome situation is a yoke. Anything attached to a person or imposed to constitute a burden or oppression is a yoke. Anything that stands as a restriction to your progress *is* a yoke. Anything that stands as a device to reduce or affect your input *is* a yoke. Any wicked device to reduce or affect your input *is* a yoke. Any evil power forcing you to a defeat *is.* a yoke. Any controlled device of the enemy against your life is a yoke. Any power that seeks to keep you in perpetual bondage is a yoke.

EXAMPLES OF BIBLICAL YOKES

The presence of Hagar in the family of Abraham *is* a yoke to Sarah and Isaac. She was an oppressive agency in the family of Abraham to despise Sarah. Her presence, like in many other polygamous families brought a lot of conflict/competition and sorrows. When a yoke agency is removed, there will be peace, thus God advised Abraham to break the yoke.

"And Sarah saw the son of Hagar the Egyptian, whom she had borne unto Abraham, mocking. Wherefore she said unto Abraham, Cast out this handmaid and her son. For the son of this handmaid shall not be heir with my son, even with Isaac. And Abraham rose up early in the morning, and took bread and a bottle of water, and gave it unto Hagar, putting it on her shoulder, and gave her the child, and sent her away. And she departed, and wandered in the wilderness of Beer-sheba" (Genesis 21:9, 10, 14).

Pharaoh the King of Egypt was an oppressive agency to the children of Israel. The yoke 'of the children of Israel in Egypt limited them and reduces the whole nation into servants. It came to a point that Pharaoh even asked a question and said who is God that I will let the children of Israel to go out of bondage? When a situation or powers begin to mock you and your God; that is a yoke.

I want to make it clear that as long as your Pharaoh is alive, you cannot succeed in life. It is either you die and your Pharaoh lives or you kill your Pharaoh and live. Pharaoh is an agent of oppression that; if you allow him, he will pursue you even across the Red Sea and kill you in your promised land. Yokes cannot just break and let you go. All that God did to Pharaoh was enough to make him to surrender but he was very obstinate, unrepentant and very unreasonable. The Lord turned their waters into blood, yet he refused to remove his yoke upon the children of Israel. Their streams, rivers and pools of waters were all affected but his yoke was not perfectly removed. There are problems like that. Everything liquid in Egypt was converted to blood but that did not change the mind of the oppressor. The Lord supplied them frogs, lice and many other plagues but he was not willing on his own to break the yoke.

Going to native doctors and herbalist does not break yokes. Purchasing prayers from commercial prophets and pastors without genuine salvation cannot break our yokes. Sacrificing to idols and praying without true repentance cannot break complex yokes.

Yokes of family Pharaoh, ancestral Pharaoh, witches and wizards are not easily broken. God went ahead to smite the entire firstborn in the land of Egypt. He started from Pharaoh's house to the captives that were in dungeons and the entire firstborn of the cattle. Yet Pharaoh was not willing to let Israel go. He pursued the children of Israel to the Red Sea where God rose and confronted him with all his trained soldiers. These things took place because Pharaoh did not want them to be freed from his yokes.

Whether you want to believe it or not, Pharaoh's victims have yokes they are identified with.

And Pharaoh said, who is the Lord, that I should obey his voice to let Israel go? I know not the Lord, neither will I let Israel go... And the king of Egypt said unto them, wherefore do ye, Moses and Aaron, let the people from their works? get you unto your burdens... Let there more work be laid upon the men, that they may labor therein; and let them not regard vain words... And the taskmasters hasted them, saying, fulfil your works, your daily tasks, as when there was straw. And the officers of the children of Israel, which Pharaoh's taskmasters had set over them, were beaten, and demanded, wherefore have ye not fulfilled your task in making brick both yesterday and today, as heretofore?... And the officers of the children of Israel did see that they were in evil case, after it was said, Ye shall not minish ought from your bricks of your daily task (Exodus 5:2, 4, 9, 13, 14, 19).

If you are waiting for your Pharaoh to break your yoke, you are wasting your time. The wickedness of Pharaoh is right inside his blood. It has no cure or remedy.

The sooner you realize that you are under a yoke and start breaking it, the better for you. The fact everyone has to know is that none can break Pharaoh's yoke without God. Sinners who despise the only true way to God would remain under their yokes.

It has been proved beyond all reasonable doubts that believers can be under yokes also. The children of Israel were delivered from Egyptian bondage. Their yokes were broken and every one of them was set free. They all sang and rejoiced, praising God for their deliverance, but one of their leaders placed another yoke upon them.

Aaron fashioned a molten calf for an image unto them. He diverted their attention from God to the molten calf. By worshipping this image, the whole nation backslid and it became a grievous yoke upon a whole nation.

As a result, their names were blotted out of God's book. The Lord left their camp and their lives were exposed to satanic attacks. The hedge of their security was broken. They were all plagued, from Aaron to the least of the people. Different sickness and calamities began to work in their midst and their lives became fertile for problem (*See Exodus 32:31-35*).

> *"And when Aaron saw it, he built an altar before it; and Aaron made proclamation, and said, Tomorrow is a feast to the LORD. And they rose up early on the morrow, and offered burnt offerings, and brought peace offerings; and the people sat down to eat and to drink, and rose up to play"* (*Exodus 32:5-6*).

Sin has been identified as the greatest yoke on mankind. Through sin many people have been yoked in different ways.

Another satanic yoke on believers is the yoke of complaint and murmuring. People of God have chosen to complain against one another instead of fighting the enemy. From the records of the bible, we see that God hates people who complained rather than praying to Him. Even if you have a problem, you are not expected to complain because doing so will fetch you more of satanic yokes. Complaints and murmurings of the children of Israel in the wilderness displeased God. As a result, many of them died in the wilderness. The fire of God was released and it burned among them. Many of them were consumed.

> "And when the people complained, it displeased the LORD: and the LORD heard it; and his anger was kindled; and the fire of the LORD burnt among them, and consumed them that were in the uttermost parts of the camp. And the people cried unto Moses; and when Moses prayed unto the LORD, the fire was quenched. And he called the name of the place Taberah: because the fire of the LORD burnt among them" (Numbers 11:1-3).

When God's fire of judgment touches a sinner, his life will not remain the same. He may purchase to himself an incurable disease that may claim his life or make life uncomfortable for him.

Satanic yokes affect a believer's journey into their promise land. Satanic yokes also cause believers to turn back from their enemies. Whenever there is transgression of God's laws, satanic yokes make the enemy to be victorious over believers. Believers are not able to withstand before their enemies. Satanic yoke can be a terrible curse in one's life.

"Israel hath sinned, and they have also transgressed my covenant which I commanded them: for they have even taken of the accursed thing, and have also stolen, and dissembled also, and they have put it even among their own stuff. Therefore, the children of Israel could not stand before their enemies, but turned their backs before their enemies, because they were accursed: neither will I be with you any more, except ye destroy the accursed from among you" (*Joshua 7:11-12*).

These are the people of God, who were once delivered from the Egyptian bondage but have now entered into another bondage.

Once a person moves away from divine ways, such one would be placed under satanic yoke. His own iniquity will take him from divine provision, and he shall be held with the cords of his sins. If he does not break such yoke, he may die under the bondage of such yoke.

> "For the ways of man are before the eyes of the LORD, and he pondereth all his goings. His own iniquities shall take the wicked himself, and he shall be holden with the cords of his sins. He shall die without instruction; and in the greatness of his folly he shall go astray" (Proverbs 5:21-23).

You cannot please God with satanic yoke in your life. Yokes of Satan limit people's productivity. Many peoples' lives are under satanic yoke because they love the things of this world. Christians who fight the battles of this life successfully must free themselves from satanic yokes.

"No man that warreth entangleth himself with the affairs of this life; that he may please him who hath chosen him to be a soldier" (2 Timothy 2:4).

From what we can see, human beings have a lot of problems that are often mysterious. Yokes take different forms. A yoke is a triangular wooden structure put on an animal that it carries about. Your type of yoke may take the form of trouble, sickness, mysterious, misfortune, affliction, unseen enemies, oppression, chronic disease, constant loss of money, mysterious loss of good job, uncontrollable desires for evil things, mysterious breakage of marriage engagements, mysterious folding of business, sudden disappearance of good helpers, unexplainable barrenness, unexplainable miscarriages, inability to conceive, acute painful menstruation, no menstruation, incurable sicknesses and their likes.

Whatever the yoke may be, the Lord is able to break it today. The pain of childbirth can go on for only few hours but the yoke of Satan can remain for a very long time.

"For it shall come to pass in that day, saith the LORD of hosts, that I will break his yoke from off thy neck, and will burst thy bonds, and strangers shall no more serve themselves of him" (*Jeremiah 30:8*).

Suffering agony, pains and trouble are what we call yokes. When you have a yoke, it is not easy to remove it yourself without God's intervention and mercy. Animals cannot on their own remove their yokes. When you expose yourself and catch a cold that is not a yoke, it is a natural thing. The yoke we are talking about is like the case of a person who is very sick having heat all over the body. Medically, he is pronounced okay but realistically, the person is dying.

Take for example the story of a man, who has no money but whenever he gets money, he forgets his problems. But as soon as the money finishes, he remembers all his problems. Yokes can make a man to lose his memory mysteriously. Think of a man who thinks too much and does not sleep.

When you see a man who never thinks about anything but at night, does not sleep, that is a real demonic yoke. A person who cannot sleep for 30 minutes unless he takes drugs is under a yoke.

"And when Herod would have brought him forth, the same night Peter was sleeping between two soldiers, bound with two chains: and the keepers before the door kept the prison" (Acts 12:6).

Herod was a great king, an enemy of God who was

determined to destroy Peter. One thing we should understand very well is that the devil is not an idiot. Read verse 6 gradually again and see how Peter was chained down. He was chained and bound with two soldiers watching him left and right. The doors were locked properly. Keepers were stationed before the door of the prison. Even when the chains fell off his hand, he still needed to pass through the first and the second wards while, the Iron Gate that led to the city was still under heavy lock with keys.

Many people's chain has already been broken but they are still in prison. They are born-again, but parts of their lives are not released. Their marriage, health, business, careers and breakthroughs are under surveillance by the enemy. They know they are not supposed to be poor but they are poor. May be what you need now is a true church, a good teacher, a deliverance minister, specific prayer points, a continued prayer to break yoke or a divine guide to lead them out of the prison to the gate that leads to the city of their destiny.

"And, behold, the angel of the Lord came upon him, and a light shined in the prison: and he smote Peter on the side, and raised him up, saying, Arise up quickly. And his chains fell off from his hands. And the angel said unto him, gird thyself, and bind on thy sandals. And so, he did. And he saith unto him, cast thy garment about thee, and follow me. And he went out, and followed him; and wist not that it was true which was done by the angel; but thought he saw a vision. When they were past the first and the second ward, they came unto the iron gate that leadeth unto the city; which opened to them of his own accord: and they went out, and passed on through one street; and forthwith the angel departed from him. And when Peter was come to himself, he said, Now I know of a surety, that the Lord hath sent his angel, and hath delivered me out of the hand of Herod, and from all the expectation of the people of the Jews" (Acts 12:7-11).

Some return to their dead churches where demons that yoked them are waiting for them, people after their deliverance from such yokes. They return to the world and to their old ways of sinful lifestyles. They treat their churches like a hospital where they go and receive doctor's assistance only for their problems to return later.

You need to remain under the fire of God and in a place where you can be fed well with true Word of God. Before certain people could pass through the iron gate, they must have knowledge of the Word of God. You need to have knowledge of the bible. You need to be involved in God's Word no matter how small. You need to be part of a true bible believing church, a ministry of Christ.

WHAT OF THE IRON GATE?

Write down the names of people am going to mention here. Write down prayers you need to pray as it affects your own life and destiny. The reason is because I may not be able to write down here in this book all the prayers you need to pray. You are in better position to discover yourself than anyone, including myself.

Has your marriage passed through the Iron Gate? Has your health passed through the Iron Gate? Joseph was a leader inside the prison. His leadership needs to pass through the Iron Gate. Many children of God are only enjoying partial deliverance. Many are delivered but things that will make them happy in life have not been delivered.

Hannah was a true child of God. She led a pure life and passed through character deliverance but her conception needed to pass through the Iron Gate that led to the city. She saw the need, prayed and fasted and God delivered her from barrenness.

Eli was a man of God; a priest of God. He was mightily

led by God to preserve the life of one of the greatest prophets in the Bible, Samuel. However, his own children's characters needed to be prayed across the Iron Gate that led to the city. Many believers' yokes have been broken yet they allow Herod to meet them inside the prison yard.

Herod did not spare any Christian or child of God, but they can fight effectively and win every battle outside the prison. Joseph must fight but that had to be outside the prison. Joseph can only care for his brethren and welcome them in Egypt for safety outside the Iron Gate. You cannot stay behind the bar and achieve God's purpose for your life. There is no way he could become a prime minister while still behind the Iron Gate. His destiny had to pass through the Iron Gate.

It is true that God anointed David to be the King of Israel, but as long as Saul was still alive, he could not sit on the throne. He may kill one thousand Goliaths, but Saul must die before his kingship commences. His prayers must pass through the Iron Gate that led unto the city gate.

If you allow your Pharaoh to be alive, your Israel will not cross the red sea. If Elijah was not taken, Elisha must forget the crown of a double portion anointing. Jehoshaphat must go into the battlefield before his enemies would leave him alone. Your prayers must pass your destiny through the Iron Gate that leads into the city of God.

If Hezekiah refused to pray and break the yoke of death, he would have died fifteen years before his time. He needed to break the yoke of death and pray himself out of the prison through the gate that led into the city.

If you are born in sorrow, Jabez was also born in sorrow and poverty characterized his life and everybody in his family line. He prayed and broke the chains of sorrow and poverty. God enlarged his coast and blessed him indeed.

Peter would have died in prison but because of prayers of the saints, he crossed the first and second wardens and came into the Iron Gate that led into the city. If you pray the prayers in this book faithfully, plus the ones you are going to write down, your destiny will get into the city of God where every provision of life is stored.

Elijah prayed and fire came down from heaven. His prayers overcame the evil powers of hell. The powers of the air could not stand his prayers. His yokes were broken and abundant rain came.

The yoke of death was upon the children of Israel in the days of king Ahasuerus and Haman. Esther and Mordecai prayed and their prayers broke the yoke and the whole nation passed through the Iron Gate that led into the City.

What are the yokes of bondage holding you, your family and people around you? Write then down and plan on how to go into prayer assault against your enemy. You can pray like Mordecai and Esther. The prayers of Daniel conquered all his enemies, including the lions in the den. What has your prayer done to Satan?

The prayers of Cain reduced his curse. The prayers of Abraham made him the father of Isaac at an old age. The prayers of Ishmael provided a well of water for him and her mother in the wilderness. The prayers of Abraham's servant lead him to choose the right wife for Isaac. The prayers of Jacob changed his name from Jacob to Israel. The prayers of Moses made Pharaoh and his entire magician to bow down to God's request. His prayers divided the Red Sea, changed bitter water to sweet water and produced manner from heaven. He took decision and approached Pharaoh and spoke to his face, "Let my people go." Since you started praying, what are the results of your prayers?

Moses took a decision not to compromise with Pharaoh's evil request. He was not tired or afraid of approaching Pharaoh to release God's people. When they were marching out from Egypt, he took the bones of Joseph. Have you ever taken anything out from the kingdom of darkness? What your father and ancestors handed over to Satan through evil sacrifices is still waiting for a warrior to rescue them.

Moses prayed and his sister's leprosy was healed. Moses fought and defeated the Amalekites. Moses destroyed the idol that Aaron made. Moses prayed for a successor and

God gave him Joshua. If your prayers have not succeeded before, they will begin to succeed in the name of Jesus. The prayer points in this book are designed to break all your evil yokes.

Our God is not a partial God. He promised to answer our prayers. Gideon prayed and God answered him. Jephthah prayed and God answered him and gave him victory. Samson prayed and God answered him. Blind Bartimaeus prayed and God answered him and opened his eyes. The lepers prayed and Jesus healed them. Cornelius prayed and God answered his prayers. No matter how stubborn your yoke may be, they shall be broken in the name of Jesus.

Do not ever joke with this program. Use this book in your hand to break into your greatness through prayers. If you finish praying the prayers in this part one, go for the part two and three of this book.

"And I will make with them a covenant of peace, and will cause the evil beasts to cease out of the land: and

they shall dwell safely in the wilderness, and sleep in the woods. And I will make them and the places round about my hill a blessing; and I will cause the shower to come down in his season; there shall be showers of blessing. And the tree of the field shall yield her fruit, and the earth shall yield her increase, and they shall be safe in their land, and shall know that I am the LORD, when I have broken the bands of their yoke, and delivered them out of the hand of those that served themselves of them" (Ezekiel 34:25-27).

The Lord has promised and He will fulfill His promises. Even problems that have the strength of long life like Methuselah will die during this program. The kings that want you to die in the bondage of Egypt will die in your place. Anything that needs to die for your life to be set free must die. Evil yokes of your life must be broken. If the sons of Lot were able to kill the giants occupying their land, then you can do much more than the sons of Lot. You are better than the sons of Lot. You are a seed of Abraham. Abraham's blessings are yours.

"That also was accounted a land of giants: giants dwelt therein in old time; and the Ammonites call them Zamzummims; A people great, and many, and tall, as the Anakims; but the LORD destroyed them before them; and they succeeded them, and dwelt in their stead: As he did to the children of Esau, which dwelt in Seir, when he destroyed the Horims from before them; and they succeeded them, and dwelt in their stead even unto this day: And the Avims which dwelt in Hazerim, even unto Azzah, the Caphtorims, which came forth out of Caphtor, destroyed them, and dwelt in their stead" (<u>Deuteronomy 2:20-23</u>).

Every yoke of your bondage will be broken. You will possess your possession and the name of Christ will be glorified in your life. If you really repent and seriously pray the prayers in the book, all your stubborn problems will vanish.

CHAPTER 2

DIFFERENT KINDS OF YOKE

In the family of evil yokes, we have many kinds. But we shall take them one after the other.

YOKE OF THE NECK

The neck is the part of the body between the head and the shoulders. When a yoke is placed upon the neck. It affects every other part of the body and makes life uncomfortable. When a wicked person takes your neck spiritually to an evil altar and yoked it, it may be impossible for you to get to your life's destination. The journey of this life would be too difficult for you. We are talking about spiritual things. The scriptures also talked about yoke of the neck. When a person's neck is spiritual yoked, he may not be able to turn to the right direction in life.

The yoke would misguide such a person and limits him to meet with wrong people. People under this yoke live all their lives serving others. They spend their lives on earth serving strangers. The yoke on their necks drives them to where their enemies needed them and not where God needs them.

"For it shall come to pass in that day, saith the LORD of hosts, that I will break his yoke from off thy neck, and will burst thy bonds, and strangers shall no more serve themselves of him" (Jeremiah 30:8).

Many traditional customs and church doctrines have

been used to divert many people. They live their lives serving the devil and their leaders. They are reduced to perpetual slaves. They fear customs, traditions and doctrines of their churches more than the Word of God. They place on people burdens and keep their victims in fear with their evil prophecies.

"Now therefore why tempt ye God, to put a yoke upon the neck of the disciples, which neither our fathers nor we were able to bear?" (Acts 15:10).

These people wanted to bring strange doctrine into the church upon the neck of the disciples.

"And certain men which came down from Judaea taught the brethren, and said, except ye be circumcised after the manner of Moses, ye cannot be saved" (Acts 15:1).

Yoke of the neck is a satanic design to take people away from God, His promises and plans. Once you accept any satanic doctrine, your religion would be in vain. It is a yoke that no one can bear and still do what God expects from him. Yoke is a device of the enemy to reduce you into a servant for life. When your brother, master, relative, friend or any evil person uses the instrument of evil yoke of the neck, you would live your life serving others. Occult people are experts in using this yoke against others through evil sacrifices, sexual intercourse and all manner of sin.

"And by thy sword shalt thou live, and shalt serve thy brother; and it shall come to pass when thou shalt have the dominion, that thou shalt break his yoke from off thy neck" (Genesis 27:40).

We are talking about a visible yoke that men know. It is

more spiritual than physical. It is an action of the wicked in agreement with spirit beings. When they summon a person to their altars, they yoke such a person with the purpose of enslaving the victim.

Esau was yoked to serve Jacob. The religious people of the days of the disciples from Judah taught the brethren that except they are circumcised after the manner of Moses, they couldn't be saved. Traditions that offer contradictory conditions before marriage can take place are yokes that would be used by Satan to destroy the marriage eventually. Any tradition that contradicts the Bible is a device to control the destinies of those who observe them. Any custom that mandates people to go contrary to the scriptures is a device to yoke people so as to control their lives. Yoke of the neck is a very dangerous yoke that needs to be broken urgently.

False doctrines, prophecies, teachings, customs and traditions are all instruments of evil yokes. Yokes make their victims not to stand up among their age grades. It makes people to look down on them. But when God breaks the bands of your yoke, you would look upright.

You can stand up and talk when others are talking. You would know your rights and stand for yourself and your people.

"I am the LORD your God, which brought you forth out of the land of Egypt, that ye should not be their bondmen; and I have broken the bands of your yoke, and made you go upright" (Leviticus 26:13).

You can stand up and say what you like and everybody would say 'Amen.' You can decree a thing and it shall be established unto you. When the bands of your yokes are broken, your enemies would rise up and support you. When the bands of your yokes are broken, you will have results and people will rally around you. When the bands of your yokes are broken, you will see your Egyptians no more. When the bands of your yokes are broken, you will be able to walk with God like Enoch. When the bands of your yokes are broken, you will be able to escape the flood like Noah.

When the bands of your yokes are broken, your Abraham will be able to leave his father's land. When the bands of your yokes are broken, you will be able to live a holy life like Abraham. Your life will be circumcised and purified. When the bands of your yokes are broken, you will be able to receive angelic visitation and ministration as it was for Abraham. When the bands of your yokes are broken, your losses shall be recovered and no Abimelech will sleep with your wife. Marriage will be made easy and you will be fruitful. When the bands of your yokes are broken, your Esau will throw away his weapons of war and embrace your Jacob in reconciliation. When the bands of your yokes are broken, your Laban will release your Jacob.

Even if you are in the prison yard, as soon as the bands of your yokes get broken, Pharaoh will call your Joseph out of every prison and promote him. Once the band of your yoke breaks, your Joseph will come out of the prison yard.

When the bands of Peter's yoke of fear broke, he started walking on top of the sea with Jesus. When the bands of

By Prayer M. Madueke

the yoke of Mary Magdalene broke, she was delivered and seven evil spirits left her. When the bands of the children of Israel in captivity were broken, king Cyrus made a proclamation and gave charge that God's house be built and the children of Israel return to their land. When the bands of the yoke of iniquity of the people of Nineveh were broken, they believed God, repented and God blessed them. When the bands of yoke of poverty, famine and destruction were broken in the life of the widow of Zerephath, she was fed together with her only son from the heavenly kitchen until the day God brought rain back into Israel. When the band of yoke in your life breaks, people around you will know. People around you will see it. People around you will testify it. Your heavens will open and you will be blessed abundantly.

"And the tree of the field shall yield her fruit, and the earth shall yield her increase, and they shall be safe in their land, and shall know that I am the LORD, when I have broken the bands of their yoke, and delivered them out of the hand of those that served themselves of them"

(*Ezekiel 34:27*).

YOKE OF IRON

Iron is a hard metal that is used to make steel. The yoke of iron is one of the most dangerous and wicked yokes of Satan. When the occult people make a sacrifice to place someone under an iron yoke and prayers are not offered to arrest it, it will cause a dangerous harm. The yoke of iron is one of the extreme ways of destroying the destiny of great people.

While the yokes of the neck make people to serve their brothers, relatives, friends and so on, the yoke of iron are specially designed to bring people to serve under their archenemies. The yoke of iron makes people to serve in hunger and in thirst and in nakedness and in want of all things. The yoke of iron is the yoke of destruction unto death

"Therefore, shalt thou serve thine enemies which the

LORD shall send against thee, in hunger, and in thirst, and in nakedness, and in want of all things: and he shall put a yoke of iron upon thy neck, until he have destroyed thee" (<u>Deuteronomy 28:48</u>).

The yoke of iron is extremely destructive. The yokes of iron are not easily broken. Other yokes can be broken by minor prayers and fasting, but the yoke of iron is a very hard yoke. The powers backing up the yoke of iron are not ready to give up willingly. No sacrifice can turn their face away from their victims. Yoke of iron can control a whole nation. Other yokes are limited to some extent but the yoke of iron has no boundary. There are yokes limited to individuals, families, institutions and organizations. But the yoke of iron has no boundary or geographical restriction.

Languages are not barriers to the yokes of iron. The yoke of iron is a merciless yoke. It does not pity its victims. It is a yoke of death. When it uses hunger against its victims and nobody would bring supply. It is a hunger to death. It is yoke of hunger that could affect someone spiritually, physically, financially, socially, academically, materially and mentally. It destroys people's homes. It is a yoke that takes the good things you already have and prevents any good thing that will try to come in. It is a yoke that opens the door of a victim to any form of evil and closes it against the good ones. It is a yoke of thirst, nakedness and wants for all things until full destruction is recorded.

No human power or knowledge can break the yoke of iron. It is a national and international yoke. It is a worldwide yoke. It is a yoke that brings evil prosperity to evil earthly kings. It is a yoke of occultism. It is a yoke that gather people together for destruction.

"Go and tell Hananiah, saying, thus saith the LORD; Thou hast broken the yokes of wood; but thou shalt make for them yokes of iron. For thus saith the LORD of hosts, the God of Israel; I have put a yoke of iron upon the neck of all these nations, that they may serve

Nebuchadnezzar king of Babylon; and they shall serve him: and I have given him the beasts of the field also" (*Jeremiah 28:13-14*).

This is the yoke that leads people into common error. This is the yoke that influences nations to forbid the use of the Bible in their nations or in particular sections like schools, families, organizations and sects. This is the yoke that gathers people into Egypt and refuses to allow them to go free. It is the yoke that binds people together under one government without a true God. It is the yoke that seeks to arrest all that is good and corrupt them in a foreign nation with false worship. It is the yoke that compels a righteous man to travel down to Egypt without seeking the face of God.

"And there was a famine in the land: and Abram went down into Egypt to sojourn there; for the famine was grievous in the land. And it came to pass, when he was come near to enter into Egypt, that he said unto Sarai

his wife, Behold now, I know that thou art a fair woman to look upon: Therefore it shall come to pass, when the Egyptians shall see thee, that they shall say, This is his wife: and they will kill me, but they will save thee alive. Say, I pray thee, thou art my sister: that it may be well with me for thy sake; and my soul shall live because of thee. And it came to pass, that, when Abram was come into Egypt, the Egyptians beheld the woman that she was very fair" (<u>Genesis 12:10-14</u>).

This is the yoke that makes people to marry many wives. This is the yoke that took Lot and his family to Sodom where they were destroyed with all their investments. This is the yoke that held the children of Israel and refused to let them go. It is also the yoke of oppression. This is the yoke that makes people to boast against God. But thanks to God who has the power to destroy every yoke.

"Thus, saith the LORD; They also that uphold Egypt shall fall; and the pride of her power shall come down: from the tower of Syene shall they fall in it by the sword, saith the Lord GOD. And I will set fire in Egypt: Sin shall have great pain, and No shall be rent asunder, and Noph shall have distresses daily. At Tehaphnehes also the day shall be darkened, when I shall break there the yokes of Egypt: and the pomp of her strength shall cease in her: as for her, a cloud shall cover her, and her daughters shall go into captivity. Thus, will I execute judgments in Egypt: and they shall know that I am the LORD" (Ezekiel 30:6, 16, 18-19).

"Thus, speaketh the LORD of hosts, the God of Israel, saying, I have broken the yoke of the king of Babylon. ⁴And I will bring again to this place Jeconiah the son of Jehoiakim king of Judah, with all the captives of Judah, that went into Babylon, saith the LORD: for I will break the yoke of the king of Babylon" (Jeremiah 28:2, 4).

This yoke is the yoke that the King of Babylon used

against all nations. Once this yoke is broken, the captive goes away from bondage. But only God can break this yoke. Occult men and false prophets like Hananiah cannot break the yoke of Babylon. It is the yoke of iron so only God can break it.

"And Hananiah spake in the presence of all the people, saying, Thus, saith the LORD; Even so will I break the yoke of Nebuchadnezzar king of Babylon from the neck of all nations within the space of two full years. And the prophet Jeremiah went his way" (Jeremiah 28:11).

A nation, kings or individuals with a yoke of iron tend to swallow every other person or nation. They use force to bring people under bondage. They use scrupulous means or laws to bring people under their bondage. Once you become a victim by any means, they will place their yoke on you, which is a yoke unto death. They can use sickness, sin, oppression, hunger and poverty of all sorts and even thirst to destroy you to death. They use all that God creates to fight their victims. They can use the elements - the sun, the moon, galaxies and stars. Human life does not mean anything to them. They can also cause severe destruction. They are in the air, seas, earth and they want to be anywhere but it is not possible. Their only problem is God and His children. So, repent, forsake your sins and join us to fight against the yoke of Iron.

THE YOKE OF OXEN

Oxen are a bull, a male cow that has been castrated. That is to say that its sex organs are removed. An ox is used in the past to pull farm equipment.

To castrate means to deprive of the testes. It also means to deprive of the ovaries or to render impotent. it also means to deprive of vitality.

When an occult person sees a great-destined person they will know. They know the people who have great stars in life. In most cases, they will castrate the person's destiny by placing the yoke of oxen on them. Many people today are spiritually castrated by the wicked people around them. When an occult personality wants to deal with a great star, destined person; they will summon them to their evil altars. If they appear, they will offer some sacrifices according to their laws and place a yoke of an ox on such a person. Once a person received the yoke into his life, an ox spiritually, he will not be physical productive. He will be deprived of his testes, ovaries and vitality and will be rendered impotent.

The doctors will examine them and find them to be perfectly okay and yet they will not be productive physically. Their input is spiritually siphoned and shared among the occult grand masters. They may not conceive or impregnate anyone because they are spiritually evacuated. The best the doctor can see is low span count, fibroid, etc., but they will not be able to give solution. People with yokes of oxen will labor in this life without achieving anything. If they get children physically, their children will be used against them. Such people may not marry at all. But if they are allowed to marry, they will marry their enemies. Satan will use their partner to torment them, days and nights.

All the mad people in the world are under the yoke of oxen. People can be partiality castrated or completely castrated under the yoke of oxen. When a castrated oxen-yoked people become mad, it means that their brain is the focus of attack. It could be on their marriage, business, health, academics but whichever place, they normally go to the extreme. The purpose of the yoke of oxen upon any human being is to reduce the person to the level of an animal, in order to waste their lives partially or completely.

Like I said before, an ox was used to pull or carry farm equipment in the past. Likewise, an occult man can summon a person to an evil altar, satanic temple and place a yoke of oxen upon such a person. Once this is done, the person will be castrated spiritually and can be diverted to the wish of his attackers. They will begin to use such a person to do anything they like. Nobody is created to be useless. Even when you are not useful to yourself, you are useful to somebody somewhere. A mad person can be the power that is carrying a prosperous mark from the family, village or even a nation. You may be the engine supplying power to a prosperous business around you. Nobody is useless at all; you are useful somewhere but you may be useful wrongly. You may be a source of power to a political heavy weight in your country. People may look at you and say, you are uselessly or a brainwashed, but truly you may be the greatest destined person in your country but you are diverted. The yoke of oxen can be used against you. This is the yoke that is ruling all over the black African continent. While the Americans, the European and other developed countries are specialized in using iron yokes, the Africans are champions of the yokes of oxen.

During the general election in Nigeria, in 2003, while I was a Pastor at one of the States, some people with guns visited a particular hospital. They took all the children in that hospital by force and probably used them for rituals. A particular woman who got married for so many years without a child but was later blessed by the Lord was there with her only child of her old age. She could not bear it; she confronted those wicked men, but they mercilessly shut her down and still went out with her only child. The blood and lives of many people have been wasted in Africa to provide for occult men to make them financial political heavy weights. You may be a victim even now.

A man was famous according as he had lifted up axes upon the thick trees (Psalms 74:5).

With the yoke of oxen upon your life, someone can use you to carry his farm equipment. You may be the source of the prosperity of the richest man in your community. You may be the oxen that are yoked to carry all the investment of the occult grandmasters in your city. It has happened to many people but you can decide that you will not be a victim. Even if you are a victim, repenting, confessing and forsaking your sins can deliver you. If you are a Christian already, you can enter into the battlefield by praying the prayers in this book and God will rescue you and break every yoke. It is possible, it can be now.

"And it came to pass, as we went to prayer, a certain damsel possessed with a spirit of divination met us, which brought her masters much gain by soothsaying" (*Acts 16:16*).

This is an example of someone under the bondage of the yoke of oxen. This lady may be destined to be a great minister of the gospel, a teacher of international repute, a medical scientist, a nurse or an ambassador but she is now reduced to a mere diviner, making many occult grandmaster's very rich by her sooth saying. The occult grandmaster of her days discovered her greatness and placed a yoke of oxen upon her. This lady was not thinking about marriage, academic, her personal welfare nor that of her parents. And her sweats, labor are unknown to her and the people around were channeled to enrich all the occult grand masters of her generation. According to the scriptures, only God and those occult grandmasters knew what was going on. You may not know who you are, or understanding why everything is turning against you. But some people know. God is aware of all the wickedness against you.

The occult grand masters of her generation knew that the damsel was the source and the hope of their gains. They knew that if the yoke of the oxen upon her is broken, their business, popularity, knowledge and recognition would be gone.

"And when her masters saw that the hope of their gains was gone, they caught Paul and Silas, and drew them into the marketplace unto the rulers" (<u>Acts 16:19</u>).

You better do everything possible to break the yoke of the oxen upon your life. There are people who have been pregnant for many years now. That is, a yoke of the oxen? The occult personalities tying those wombs know that once that baby is born, it will be the end of their gains. The babies in those wombs may be destined to be great, hence the occult grand masters have tied them and prevented their birth. There are so many testimonies you have not given birth to. But I believe God that as you pray these prayers, your destinies will be born as you break the yoke of oxen in your life. Don't allow anyone to reduce you to the level of an animal. Don't allow your real person to be locked up.

"And call ye on the name of your gods, and I will call on the name of the LORD: and the God that answereth by fire, let him be God. And all the people answered and said, it is well spoken. And it came to pass at the time of the offering of the evening sacrifice, that Elijah the prophet came near, and said, LORD God of Abraham, Isaac, and of Israel, let it be known this day that thou art God in Israel, and that I am thy servant, and that I have done all these things at thy word. Then the fire of the LORD fell, and consumed the burnt sacrifice, and the wood, and the stones, and the dust, and licked up the water that was in the trench" (<u>1 Kings 18:24</u>, <u>36</u>, <u>38</u>).

This is not time to halt between two opinions, we need to really go into battlefield. It is better to die while fighting a good fight than to be alive, making gains for the enemies of God. God forbids that I will be placed under the yoke of oxen. I refuse to be a waste product, an unproductive personality in the kingdom of God. The yoke of oxen in anyone's life, makes the person useless and unprofitable to himself, but profitable and productive to others, to the glory of Satan. We must try and fight to break the yoke of the oxen placed upon us by anybody. Some parents can place a yoke of oxen from their linage. Sin can also place on anybody, in any nation of the world, the yoke of oxen. But no matter the type of yoke you have, God can break them.

"And it shall come to pass in that day, that his burden shall be taken away from off thy shoulder, and his yoke from off thy neck, and the yoke shall be destroyed because of the anointing" (Isaiah 10:27).

1 know a lady in one of the universities in Africa. A few years ago, her father served the queen of heaven. So, she grew up and found herself serving in satanic temples and shrines. Her father was a grand master under the kingdom of the Queen of Heaven.

"Then all the men which knew that their wives had burned incense unto other gods, and all the women that stood by, a great multitude, even all the people that dwelt in the land of Egypt, in Pathros, answered Jeremiah, saying, As for the word that thou hast spoken unto us in the name of the LORD, we will not hearken unto thee. But we will certainly do whatsoever thing goeth forth out of our own mouth, to burn incense unto the queen of heaven, and to pour out drink offerings unto her, as we have done, we, and our fathers, our kings, and our princes, in the cities of Judah, and in the streets of Jerusalem: for then had we plenty of victuals, and were well, and saw no evil. But since we left off to burn incense to the queen of heaven, and to pour out drink offerings unto her, we have wanted all things, and have been consumed by the sword and by the famine" (Jeremiah 44:15-18).

This lady in question was a determined person who vowed never to defile herself and therefore, remained a virgin. Before her father died, he handed her over to her cousin who is grandmaster, directly working with Lucifer.

Her cousin started taking good care of her; even to the university level. One day, the man called her and informed her that it was time for her to work with some spirits beings. Because she is a virgin; she was highly needed in the occult world. There are sacrifices that only a virgin can perform to Lucifer which no other person can offer; including the highest occultist in the whole world. There are also levels of virginity among virgins. There are virgins that have allowed human hands and other objects to enter their bodies. These are virgins who have defiled breasts. 'There are also pure virgins; whose bodies have not been touched by men nor seen by men from their adult age. All I am saying is that; there are a category of virgins and the occultist does not joke with them. An occult man can do everything possible to secure the service of such virgins as a temple girl

They can spend any amount of money to keep such ladies unmarried. They can castrate such people because they are not easy to be found in our generation. God also is looking for such men and women. When He found the Virgin Mary; He used her to bless the whole world.

The Occult man in question has done everything possible and he was full of confidence that he has gotten a temple girl. But to his greatest surprise, the girl turned down his request. He did everything possible but the lady bluntly refused. He looked at the lady and said to her; I have been faithful to Lucifer in all aspect. I have never failed in all assignment he has assigned to me and in this one, I will not fail him. He assured the lady that if she insisted that even Jesus Christ would not deliver her from his hands.

That was how the battle started. A few weeks later; while the lady was in an examination hall; all her properties got burnt. All her helpers were removed and everybody was against her. The occult man used everything God created to fight against her. Her spinal cord; her brain; her sight; her academics, her menses and everything you can think of were against her.

Anybody that wanted to assist her faced one disaster or one thing and another that made it impossible for her to be assisted. The few remaining helpers; including her own blood relations demanded defilement before they could assist her. It was so bad that she felt abandoned and rejected. She began to have all manner of mysterious problem and while all these things were taking place; the occult man was sending messages to her, telling her that she could come and have anything she wanted in life when she is tired. Every door of escape seems to close; as the occult man normally appeared to anyone who wished to assist her in the dream. Some helpers who insisted, lost their jobs or faced one mysterious problem or the other.

To cut a long story; the lady stood her ground and today; she is a qualified medical doctor instead of a temple girl. You can be a temple boy or a girl without knowing it. You may be working for Satan without any letter of appointment. Your office may be in the temple of Lucifer or the altar of the Queen of Heaven, queen of the coast and yet think that you are serving God.

You may be spiritually castrated and your destiny may be deposited in satanic temple. It is better to die than to be a temple girl/boy, man or woman. The yoke of oxen is a local yoke that has been expanded to international level. That *is* to say, they are of different levels.

"I will also break in pieces with thee the shepherd and his flock; and with thee will I break in pieces the husbandman and his yoke of oxen; and with thee will I break in pieces captains and rulers" (<u>*Jeremiah 51:23*</u>).

"And he returned back from him, and took a yoke of oxen, and slew them, and boiled their flesh with the instruments of the oxen, and gave unto the people, and they did eat. Then he arose, and went after Elijah, and ministered unto him" (<u>*1 Kings 19:21*</u>).

We can also see a single yoke of oxen on display in (*1 Samuel 11:7*).

We can see a personalized oxen yoke in (*1 Kings 19:21*).

"And he took a yoke of oxen, and hewed them in pieces, and sent them throughout all the coasts of Israel by the hands of messengers, saying, whosoever cometh not forth after Saul and after Samuel, so shall it be done unto his oxen. And the fear of the LORD fell on the people, and they came out with one consent" (<u>1 Samuel 11: 7</u>).

In 1 Kings 19:19, we see 12 yokes of oxen. In (Luke 14:19), we see 5 yokes of oxen. In (Job 42:12), we see one thousand yokes of oxen. In (Job 1:3), we see 5 thousand yokes of oxen.

One yoke of oxen can be used to hold a person's destiny. It can also be used to hold more people. An occult personality can use a single sacrifice to yoke a whole family, village, city or nation. One occult person can have more people under *his* custody just with one yoke.

"His substance also was seven thousand sheep, and three thousand camels, and five hundred yoke of oxen, and five hundred she asses, and a very great household; so that this man was the greatest of all the men of the east" (Job 1:3).

Is your marriage, business, health, breakthroughs, family etc, under a yoke? They can be delivered today. The anointing can break the yokes. The prayers in this book are the prayers of anointing. Each prayer point carries an irresistible anointing that can break every yoke.

GRIEVOUS OR HEAVY YOKE

To be grieved means to be burdened or to be heavy with deep sorrow. It means to cause someone to suffer or to be under distress. It means to feel grief or sorrow.

Grievousness is caused or characterized by severe pain; suffering or sorrow as a result of wound, loss or oppression.

Heavy yoke carries great weight that weighs down its victims. It is very difficult and hard to bear a heavy yoke.

Heavy yoke is also burdensome. It causes its victim to be pregnant with problem all through life. Heavy yoke deals with its victims to suffer beyond moderation. It is a load heavier than the carrier cumbrous; cumbersome; and bulky and hinders free movement.

A heavy yoke is a device by the occult and wicked people to give people the problem that they cannot bear.

Solomon made the normal yoke of the children of Israel to increase beyond normal. When a problem defiles medical solution; it is regarded as abnormal and grievous. When other people's problem goes in a program or after the same level of prayer or medical treatment; but yours still remains; such problems are regarded as heavy or grievous.

Grievous or heavy yokes make problems to last longer than necessary. When you pray a normal dose of prayer or take normal drugs but the problem still remains, it is a heavy or grievous yoke. Heavy yokes prevent its victims from giving attention to any other thing. It keeps her victims in a place and demands full attention. This is the yoke that physically paralyze a person. When you see a person, who is confined to a wheel chair, such a person is suffering under grievous or heavy yoke. When you see someone, whose legs are amputated as a result of one accident or the other, that is a grievous or heavy yoke.

When you see an industrious; busy person before but who is now bed ridden as a result of sickness; which is an action from the yoke of heaviness. Any situation that wastes someone's life is a heavy yoke. When you see a chain smoker that has problem and yet is not ready to stop smoking; he is under a heavy yoke.

Any habit that someone wishes to stop but finds it difficult or almost impossible; it is a grievous yoke. When you see anyone that is rendered half dead and half alive; it is a grievous yoke.

When you know what you supposed to do; and wish to do it; but you are not able; it is a grievous and a heavy yoke. When you have a responsibility but you are being prevented by some powers; it is a grievous yoke. When others whom you are better than put a little effort and succeed; but you are not able to succeed despite all your efforts; you have a heavy and grievous yoke. If a particular condition or problem takes all that you get in life; it is a grievous yoke. When you are supposed to marry; but you are not able to marry. it is a grievous yoke. When you have all that it takes in life to succeed but yet you cannot; you are under a heavy yoke. When you have a child; parents; or wife that almost all you get goes in into him; and yet there is nothing to show for it, it is a grievous yoke.

When people treat you without a respect or mercy, it is a heavy yoke. Those who cannot control their sexual desires are under heavy yokes.

"I was wroth with my people, I have polluted mine inheritance, and given them into thine hand: thou didst shew them no mercy; upon the ancient hast thou very heavily laid thy yoke" (Isaiah 47:6).

A heavy yoked person will know exactly what to do but will not be able to do It. A grievous and heavy yoked person will see danger coming but will not be able to escape even though he wanted to. They will know what to say but they will not be able to say it. They will be in the wrong place but they will not be able to make a change. They will know that this decision for sin is wrong but they will not be able to change. They will know that a system is wrong but they will not be able to break out of it. People like this will not move forward because they are under heavy yoke.

"Thy father made our yoke grievous: now therefore make thou the grievous service of thy father, and his heavy yoke which he put upon us, lighter, and we will serve thee" (1 Kings 12:4).

When a yoke is placed upon you, you will have a burden that is beyond your strength. Only Jesus the burden bearer can deliver a person with the yoke of a burden. With such a yokel, any little thing will burden you. People with such yokes can easily be discouraged. Any little problem they will complain.

CHAPTER 3

THE YOKE OF TRANSGRESSION

Transgression is going beyond the limit of what is moral or legally acceptable to God.

"The yoke of my transgressions is bound by his hand: they are wreathed, and come up upon my neck: he hath made my strength to fall, the Lord hath delivered me into their hands, from whom I am not able to rise up" *(Lamentation 1:14).*

Yoke of transgression is the greatest evil yoke in the kingdom of darkness ever fashioned against mankind. This yoke has affected the life of every creature under the heavens, of all generations past and present. With this yoke upon anyone, he must be doing things wrong in the sight of God. Nobody will be under the yoke of transgression and live a holy life. The yoke of transgression takes one away completely from the righteousness required by God to make one reputable. Whoever has this yoke will not make it to heaven, if he falls to break it. The yoke of transgression is of many kinds, sizes and colors, depending on where you are born or your involvement in life.

Satan disgraced many great people of God who were trapped by his yoke. Only a man who is born again, living a consistent Christian life can break this yoke by God's grace. Yoke of transgression enters a man's life as soon as one is born, no matter whom they are. It is contacted by inheritance.

"Behold, I was shapen in iniquity; and in sin did my mother conceive me" (Psalms 51:5).

Nobody is free or can be free from this yoke until he realizes that he is a sinner, repents, confesses and forsakes sin. Even those who are already born again but fail to keep their salvation can be re-yoked and brought under the power of Satan. With this yoke present in the life of anybody, he is bound to transgress the law of God. The yoke of transgression is the most powerful and dangerous yoke among all the yokes of Satan.

Below are examples of people who were victims of the yoke of transgression.

This is the yoke that the enemy used against Adam and Eve. This yoke tuned their eyes, mind, thoughts and imagination towards the forbidden tree. This is the yoke that captured the desires of Eve, and made her forget all the divine instructions. This particular yoke made her to relax in an evil discussion with the greatest enemy of her life. The yoke of transgression drew everything that was in Eve towards her destruction. She saw her enemy as a good visitor. She listened to her greatest enemy, obeyed his voice, and it became a transgression unto her against the laws of God. This same yoke pulled Adam and he also ate the forbidden fruit in the Garden of Eden.

The same yoke pulled them out from the presence of God and hid them from Him. The yoke of transgression made them to argue with God and caused them to shift blame instead of repenting to break the yoke of transgression that was upon them. When they rejected repentance and preferred the yoke of transgression, God cursed them and took away his protection from them. The yoke of transgression exposes its victim to satanic attacks and breaks the hedge of security off them. Whosoever is under the bondage of the yoke of transgression is under a curse no matter how religious he may be. The yoke of transgression does not allow its victims to produce the righteousness acceptable to God. The righteousness produced by anyone under the yoke of transgression, is like the filthy rag before God.

His righteousness will not be enough to make him a child of God. The yoke of transgression is the yoke of hell. Through the yoke of transgression, every other problem can be invited into someone's life. It is the yoke of death and hell, sickness and disease.

This is the yoke that compelled Cain to kill his younger brother, Abel. It is the yoke of wrath against your fellow human being. This is the yoke that reduced Cain to a fugitive and vagabond throughout his life on earth. This is the yoke that can make people to hate their own blood relation with perfect hatred unto death. This is the yoke that made Cain stubborn and used him to ask his Creator a question without respect.

This is the yoke that makes people to marry anybody they like without asking counsel from God. This is the yoke of wickedness, evil thoughts and evil imagination without end.

"The earth also was corrupt before God, and the earth was filled with violence. And God looked upon the earth, and, behold, it was corrupt, for all flesh had corrupted his way upon the earth. And God said unto Noah, the end of all flesh is come before me; for the earth is filled with violence through them; and, behold, I will destroy them with the earth" (Genesis 6:11-13).

With this yoke upon people in any community, city, or nation, corruption and violence will characterize their actions. This is the yoke that came upon the sons of Noah and they started an evil project without divine approval. This is the yoke that affected the life of a great man like Abraham and he went down to Egypt without prayer. This yoke made him to tell lies and taught her wife to do so and their marriage was separated.

This is the yoke that made Pharaoh to take another man's wife. It is the yoke of transgression that pushes people to marry a second wife - the yoke of polygamy.

This is the yoke that made Lot to enjoy the gossips of his herdsmen and made him to separate from a man called by God. Later, he lost all that he had in life. This is the yoke that made Hagar to despise her mistress, Sarah and later, she was thrown into the wilderness with her only child to die without water. This is the yoke that wrought all the people living in Sodom and Gomorrah together to fight against God. They provoked God to use fire, like brimstone to wipe them out.

The people under the yoke of transgression did all the evil ever done upon the earth. With this yoke in this world the world can never know peace. As long as you refuse to repent and forsake your sins you are under the yoke of transgression. When this yoke came upon Pharaoh, the king of Egypt, he used it to chain the entire world under himself. This is the yoke Nebuchadnezzar used against 127 provinces all over the world and made them to abandon their Creator.

Thank God those three small houseboys - the Jewish slaves - broke their own yokes of transgression.

> *"Shadrach, Meshach, and Abed-nego, answered and said to the king, O Nebuchadnezzar, we are not careful to answer thee in this matter. But if not, be it known unto thee, O king, that we will not serve thy gods, nor worship the golden image, which thou hast set up"* (Daniel 3:16, 18).

This is the yoke that came upon the church of God in Thyatira and they enthroned a woman called Jezebel as a prophetess and she began to teach and to seduce the servants of God to commit fornication and eat things sacrificed to the idols.

> "Notwithstanding I have a few things against thee, because thou sufferest that woman Jezebel, which calleth herself a prophetess, to teach and to seduce my servants to commit fornication, and to eat things sacrificed unto idols. And I gave her space to repent of her fornication; and she repented not" (Revelation 2:20, 21).

When this yoke captured Demas, he became worldly and abandoned his God-given ministry. This is the yoke that makes people to be worldly instead of being spiritual. The yoke of transgression makes people unruly, vain deceivers and talkative.

> "For there are many unruly and vain talkers and deceivers, specially they of the circumcision" (Titus 1:10).

The yoke of transgression quickens church workers to stand against the true ministers of God in the church. Whoever rises up in the church against any true minister of God is under the yoke of transgression.

> *"Alexander the coppersmith did me much evil: The Lord reward him according to his works: at my first answer no man stood with me, but all men forsook me: I pray God that it may not be laid to their charge" (2 Timothy 4:14, 16).*

This is the yoke that converts God's creature to an enemy of God. It is a yoke that causes people to hate God.

> *"And when they had gone through the isle unto Paphos, they found a certain sorcerer, a false prophet, a Jew, whose name was Bar-jesus: But Elymas the sorcerer (for so is his name by interpretation) withstood them, seeking to turn away the deputy from the faith" (Acts 13:6, 8).*

This is the yoke that makes people to do evil business and reduce people to worship idols.

> *"Now it came to pass, after that Amaziah was come from the slaughter of the Edomites, that he brought the gods of the children of Seir, and set them up to be his gods, and bowed down himself before them, and burned incense unto them. And it came to pass, as he talked with him, that the king said unto him, Art thou made of the King's Counsel? Forbear; why shouldest thou be smitten? Then the prophet forbare, and said, I know that God hath determined to destroy thee, because thou hast done this, and hast not hearkened unto my counsel"* (2 Chronicles 25:14, 16).

The yoke of transgression makes nations to be converted to liars and boasters.

> *"We have heard of the pride of Moab; he is very proud: even of his haughtiness, and his pride, and his wrath: but his lies shall not be so"* (Isaiah 16:6).

This is the yoke that destroys the sons of the priest, if chances are given to them:

"Now the sons of Eli were sons of Belial; they knew not the LORD. And the priests' custom with the people was, that, when any man offered sacrifice, the priest's servant came, while the flesh was in seething, with a fleshhook of three teeth in his hand; And he struck it into the pan, or kettle, or caldron, or pot; all that the fleshhook brought up the priest took for himself. So, they did in Shiloh unto all the Israelites that came thither. Also, before they burnt the fat, the priest's servant came, and said to the man that sacrificed, give flesh to roast for the priest; for he will not have sodden flesh of thee, but raw. And if any man said unto him, let them not fail to burn the fat presently, and then take as much as thy soul desireth; then he would answer him, Nay; but thou shalt give it me now: and if not, I will take it by force. Wherefore the sin of the young men was very great before the LORD: for men abhorred the offering of the LORD" (1 Samuel 2:12-17).

The yoke of transgression has dealt with individuals of great and small cities and nations of the world. This is the yoke that almost destroyed the whole nations of Israel.

"And when the people complained, it displeased the LORD: and the LORD heard it; and his anger was kindled; and the fire of the LORD burnt among them, and consumed them that were in the uttermost parts of the camp. And he called the name of the place Taberah: because the fire of the LORD burnt among them" (Numbers 11:1, 3).

This is the yoke that provoked Moses and he smote the rock twice instead of speaking to it as God instructed. The yoke of transgression invited Zimri and Cozbi into an evil relationship until death destroyed both of them in one day.

This is the yoke that pushed King Solomon around women until he married seven hundred wives and three hundred concubines. This is the yoke that confused

Solomon and tuned away his heart after other gods and made his heart imperfect before God. This yoke pushed King Ahab around until he began to do evil in the sight of God above all the kings that were before him.

The yoke of transgression is a yoke of waste through unholy war. This is the yoke that was placed upon Simeon and Levi, and they deceived a whole nation of Shechem and later slew all the men of Shechem when they were sore (See Genesis 34:25-31). Jacob, their father later cursed them for this transgression.

> *"Simeon and Levi are brethren; instruments of cruelty are in their habitations. O my soul, come not thou into their secret; unto their assembly, mine honor, be not thou united: for in their anger they slew a man, and in their self-will they digged down a wall. Cursed be their anger, for it was fierce; and their wrath, for it was cruel: I will divide them in Jacob, and scatter them in Israel"* *(Genesis 49:5-7).*

This is the yoke that was placed upon Achan and he transgressed against God. This yoke of transgression affected the children of Israel and they suffered defeat from the hand of a small nation called Ai. The men of Ai smote the children of Israel and about thirty-six soldiers of them died. Because of the yoke of transgression upon Achan, Ai chased them from the gate even unto Shebarim *(See Joshua 7:1, 5).*

When this yoke is upon a person, it can draw other people around into problems.

Men who are yoked with transgression suffer defeat in battle. The nations of Philistines were under the yoke of transgression when they went to war against the children of Israel. With this yoke in the battlefield the children of the Philistines were defeated - six hundred men of them.

"And after him was Shamgar the son of Anath, which slew of the Philistines six hundred men with an ox goad: and he also delivered Israel" (Judges 3:31).

Any individual or nation with the yoke of transgression cannot win any battle of life both spiritually and physically. The Amalekites and the Medianites were under the yoke of transgression. They combined their soldiers to fight against Israel but they were defeated. In the battlefield, the Lord set every man's sword against his fellow (See *Judges 6:33; 40:7:1, 25, 8:10-13, 15, 21, 28*).

No matter how experienced you are in war, you cannot win any battle successfully with the yoke of transgression. Men and women who first break evil yokes of transgression win spiritual and physical battles. Minor problems and wars have destroyed a lot of people who are under the yoke of transgression. The woman of Thebez defeated the "undefeatable" Abimelech in war just because Abimelech refused to break the yoke of transgression.

"Then went Abimelech to Thebez, and encamped against Thebez, and took it. But there was a strong tower within the city, and thither fled all the men and women, and all they of the city, and shut it to them, and gat them up to the top of the tower. And Abimelech

came unto the tower, and fought against it, and went hard unto the door of the tower to burn it with fire. And a certain woman cast a piece of a millstone upon Abimelech's head, and all to break his skull. Then he called hastily unto the young man his armor bearer, and said unto him, draw thy sword, and slay me, that men say not of me, a woman slew him. And his young man thrust him through, and he died. And when the men of Israel saw that Abimelech was dead, they departed every man unto his place" (Judges 9:50-55).

Goliath was experienced in war. He was a giant and warrior that had never suffered defeat among the yoked soldiers. David was just a boy without any previous military experience but with the yoke of the Lord he entered into the battlefield and defeated the great Goliath. Goliath failed in war not because he was weak, but because he had the yoke of transgression upon him. David also prevailed over all the Philistines who came to the battlefield with the yoke of transgression. Nobody can win any battle successfully with the yoke of transgression in place (See 1 Samuel 17:1-11, 21-22, 38-58).

God is not a respecter of persons. When the righteous king of Judah, Josiah rejected every counsel and put upon himself the yoke of transgression and went into war against Pharaoh-nechoh, the king of Egypt. He was defeated and slain in the battlefield. No matter who you are, you cannot successfully win any battle, if the yoke of transgression is upon you.

"Notwithstanding the LORD turned not from the fierceness of his great wrath, wherewith his anger was kindled against Judah, because of all the provocations that Manasseh had provoked him withal. And his servants carried him in a chariot dead from Megiddo, and brought him to Jerusalem, and buried him in his own sepulchre. And the people of the land took Jehoahaz the son of Josiah, and anointed him, and made him king in his father's stead. Jehoahaz was twenty and three years old when he began to reign; and he reigned three months in Jerusalem. And his mother's name was Hamutal, the daughter of Jeremiah of Libnah. And he did that which was evil in the sight of the LORD,

according to all that his fathers had done" (2 Kings 23:26, 30-12).

Every occultist who wishes to defeat a righteous person in battle must use this yoke against his opponent before he fights. The children of Israel always suffered defeat when they allowed themselves to be yoked with transgression. This yoke has destroyed many righteous people who have allowed this yoke to grow roots in their lives. A wise person would not allow the yoke of transgression into his life. This is the yoke that Balaam and Balak used against the children of Israel in the wilderness and many of them died shamefully.

"And Israel abode in Shittim, and the people began to commit whoredom with the daughters of Moab. And Israel joined himself unto Baal-peor: and the anger of the LORD was kindled against Israel. And those that died in the plague were twenty and four thousand" (Numbers 25:1, 3, 9).

The yoke of transgression is the yoke of waste by death. This yoke arrested a man called Jared in the bible and he lived 961 years without any meaningful achievement. The only good thing said about him was that he fathered Enoch (See *Genesis 5:20*).

The yoke of transgression placed upon the wife of Lot allowed her to gather great wealth and build mansions in Sodom. But in the days of the battle, she as defeated and converted to a useless pillar of salt on her way of escape. She nearly made it but she was pulled back to destruction by the yoke of transgression.

"But his wife looked back from behind him, and she became a pillar of salt" (Genesis 19:26).

All the men who sought the life of Moses under the yoke of transgression failed. The yoke of transgression does not allow anyone to achieve anything upon this earth. These men wasted all their time seeking how to kill Moses – they all failed.

"And the LORD said unto Moses in Midian, Go, return into Egypt: for all the men are dead which sought thy life" (Exodus 4:19).

When the Egyptian strongmen failed to break the yoke of transgression upon them, they all died in shame. However, all the children of Israel who broke the yoke of transgression lived to testify to the goodness of God:

"And the hail smote throughout all the land of Egypt all that was in the field, both man and beast; and the hail smote every herb of the field, and break every tree of the field. Only in the land of Goshen, where the children of Israel were, was there no hail" (Exodus 9:25-26).

The entire first born of Egypt died because of the yoke of transgression. All the trained security men of Egypt were around that midnight. The soldiers of Egypt who were trained to kill could not be of help to the entire first born of Egypt under the yoke of transgression. That very midnight; from the first born of Pharaoh that sat on his throne, unto the entire first born of the captives that were in the Dungeon were slain.

> *"And it came to pass, that at midnight the LORD smote all the firstborn in the land of Egypt, from the firstborn of Pharaoh that sat on his throne unto the firstborn of the captive that was in the dungeon; and all the firstborn of cattle. And Pharaoh rose up in the night, he, and all his servants, and all the Egyptians; and there was a great cry in Egypt; for there was not a house where there was not one dead" (Exodus 12:29-30).*

> *"The Lord Himself overthrew the host of the Egyptian army who went into the midst of the sea with the yoke of transgression" (Exodus 14:22-23).*

Nobody can cross the Red Sea of his life with the yoke of transgression in his life. The yoke of transgression exposes its victims to failures and satanic attacks.

> *Anyone with this yoke is bound to have many problems that he will not be able to contend with. Twelve*

thousand soldiers of the nation of Ai were defeated and slain in battle because they came into the battlefield of life with the yoke of transgression upon them. The head of their kings was hanged in the sun till evening because he was a king with the yoke of transgression (See Joshua 8:14-29).

The ten thousand men of the Canaanites, the Perizites, and other nations were killed in the battlefield for daring to fight battles with evil yokes of transgression upon them (See Judges 1:4-8).

The seventy kings who gathered meat under the table of Adonibezek had their thumbs, and their great toes cut off by him. Adonibezek went into war with the yoke of transgression and it was done unto him what he did to the seventy kings, in payment for his sins.

"And they found Adoni-bezek in Bezek: and they fought against him, and they slew the Canaanites and the Perizzites. But Adoni-bezek fled; and they pursued after him, and caught him, and cut off his thumbs and his

great toes. And Adoni-bezek said, Threescore and ten kings, having their thumbs and their great toes cut off, gathered their meat under my table: as I have done, so God hath requited me. And they brought him to Jerusalem, and there he died" (Judges 1:5-7).

The great warrior of his generation, Sisera, died in the hands of an ordinary woman. He went into the battle with the yoke of transgression and before he knew it, Jael, the wife of Heber put her hand to the nail and a hammer in her right hand and smote him unto death, as he was fast asleep.

"She put her hand to the nail, and her right hand to the workmen's hammer; and with the hammer she smote Sisera, she smote off his head, when she had pierced and stricken through his temples. At her feet he bowed, he fell, he lay down: at her feet he bowed, he fell: where he bowed, there he fell down dead. The mother of Sisera looked out at a window, and cried through the lattice, why is his chariot so long in coming? Why tarry the

wheels of his chariots? Her wise ladies answered her, yea, she returned answer to herself, have they not sped? Have they not divided the prey; to every man a damsel or two; to Sisera a prey of divers colors, a prey of divers colors of needlework, of divers colors of needlework on both sides, meet for the necks of them that take the spoil? So, let all thine enemies perish, O LORD: but let them that love him be as the sun when he goeth forth in his might. And the land had rest forty years" (Judges 5:26-31).

This world is full of battles. Many have lost the battle of life because they failed to break the yoke of transgression. Forty-two thousand young soldiers with the yoke of transgression lost their lives, because that yoke denied them of a common pronouncement from SHIBBOLETH TO SIBBOLE1H (Judges 12:1, 6).

When your holiness is reduced as a Christian, you may be a casualty in the battlefield. When your prayer life reduces, the enemy may yoke you up with the yoke of transgression. And once a person is yoked with the yoke of transgression, he will begin to fail in every battle. And once you begin to fail in the battles of life, you may lose your life. And once you lose your life under the yoke of transgression you may go to hell fire to spend your eternity. May God forbid!

Ten thousand men went into the battlefield against one single man. In the battlefield all of them died because they were under the yoke of transgression.

"And he found a new jawbone of an ass, and put forth his hand, and took it, and slew a thousand men therewith. And Samson said, With the jawbone of an ass, heaps upon heaps, with the jaw of an ass have I slain a thousand men" (Judges 15:15-16).

The children of Israel who once broke the yoke of transgression upon them went back into sin. When they were re-yoked; four thousands of them died in the hand of their enemies including the two sons of Eli that favored the yoke of transgression.

"And the word of Samuel came to all Israel. Now Israel went out against the Philistines to battle, and pitched beside Eben-ezer: and the Philistines pitched in Aphek. And the Philistines put themselves in array against Israel: and when they joined battle, Israel was smitten before the Philistines: and they slew of the army in the field about four thousand men. And the messenger answered and said, Israel is fled before the Philistines, and there hath been also a great slaughter among the people, and thy two sons also, Hophni and Phinehas, are dead, and the ark of God is taken" (1 Samuel 4:1-2, 17).

Absalom, the son of David yoked his destiny under the yoke of transgressed and he died without a son. The tribe of Dan singled themselves out from other tribes of Israel and yoked themselves with the yoke of transgression. With that yoke upon them seventy thousand of them died in shame.

"So, the LORD sent a pestilence upon Israel from the morning even to the time appointed: and there died of

the people from Dan even to Beer-sheba seventy thousand men. And when the angel stretched out his hand upon Jerusalem to destroy it, the LORD repented him of the evil, and said to the angel that destroyed the people, it is enough: stay now thine hand. And the angel of the LORD was by the threshing place of Araunah the Jebusite. And David spake unto the LORD when he saw the angel that smote the people, and said, Lo, I have sinned, and I have done wickedly: but these sheep, what have they done? Let thine hand, I pray thee, be against me, and against my father's house" (2 Samuel 24:15-17).

No matter how close you are to God, once you allow yourself to be yoked with transgression, you will begin to fail in the battles of life and it can lead you unto death. Zimri, who refused to break the yoke of transgression upon his life suffered very well. And the yoke of transgression begin to drag him around. He committed suicide and burned the house over himself dying in a shameful manner.

"And it came to pass, when Zimri saw that the city was taken, that he went into the palace of the king's house, and burnt the king's house over him with fire, and died, For his sins which he sinned in doing evil in the sight of the LORD, in walking in the way of Jeroboam, and in his sin which he did, to make Israel to sin. Now the rest of the acts of Zimri, and his treason that he wrought, are they not written in the book of the Chronicles of the kings of Israel?" (1 Kings 16:18-20).

The yoke of transgression upon the nation of Edom brought them so low that a single man, Amaziah, slew up to ten thousand of them.

"He slew of Edom in the valley of salt ten thousand, and took Selah by war, and called the name of it Joktheel unto this day" (2 Kings 14:7).

To go into the battlefield of this life with the yoke of transgression is a very high risk. Many have lost lives and properties as a result of that. It is wise to spend time to break the yoke of transgression before doing any other thing in life. To get into marriage, business or anything with the yoke of sin transgression upon your life is the worst mistake in life. Many great nations of the world in the past tried it and failed woefully.

> *"And the king of Assyria brought men from Babylon, and from Cuthah, and from Ava, and from Hamath, and from Sepharvaim, and placed them in the cities of Samaria instead of the children of Israel: and they possessed Samaria, and dwelt in the cities thereof. And so, it was at the beginning of their dwelling there, that they feared not the LORD: therefore, the LORD sent lions among them, which slew some of them"* (2 Kings 17:24-25).

There are many problems killing people like lions today. Many sicknesses, diseases, infirmities, poverty and other things are fighting the yoked individuals, families and nations like lions today. We need to do everything possible to break the yoke of transgression before doing any other thing in life. Sennacherib tried to succeed with the yoke of transgression; but he failed. His own son slew him beside his idols.

"And it came to pass that night that the angel of the LORD went out, and smote in the camp of the Assyrians an hundred fourscore and five thousand: and when they arose early in the morning, behold, they were all dead corpses. So, Sennacherib king of Assyria departed, and went and returned, and dwelt at Nineveh. And it came to pass, as he was worshipping in the house of Nisroch his god, that Adrammelech and Sharezer his sons smote him with the sword: and they escaped into the land of Armenia. And Esar-haddon his son reigned in his stead" (2 Kings 19:35-37).

The children of Ammon, Moab and Mount Seir tried fighting with the yoke of transgression. But they ended up fighting and killing themselves.

"And when they began to sing and to praise, the LORD set ambushments against the children of Ammon, Moab, and mount Seir, which were come against Judah; and they were smitten. For the children of Ammon and Moab stood up against the inhabitants of mount Seir, utterly to slay and destroy them: and when they had made an end of the inhabitants of Seir, every one helped to destroy another. And when Judah came toward the watchtower in the wilderness, they looked unto the multitude, and, behold, they were dead bodies fallen to the earth, and none escaped. And when Jehoshaphat and his people came to take away the spoil of them, they found among them in abundance both riches with the dead bodies, and precious jewels, which they stripped off for themselves, more than they could carry away: and they were three days in gathering of the spoil, it was so much" (2 Chronicles 20:22-25).

The yoke of transgression set people against themselves, and make people to get confused in life. This was the yoke that deceived Uzziah and killed him as a leper.

"Now the rest of the acts of Uzziah, first and last, did Isaiah the prophet, the son of Amoz, write. So Uzziah slept with his fathers, and they buried him with his fathers in the field of the burial which belonged to the kings; for they said, He is a leper: and Jotham his son reigned in his stead" (2 Chronicles 26:22-23).

You cannot be under this yoke and make it in life. It is not possible at all.

The mighty men of Assyria who were noted for war and victories failed. They remained under this yoke and they were still winning every battle. God himself sent a single Angel who slew about 175,000 of them in a single night.

"And the LORD sent an angel, which cut off all the mighty men of valor, and the leaders and captains in the camp of the king of Assyria. So, he returned with shame of face to his own land. And when he was come into the house of his god, they that came forth of his own bowels slew him there with the sword. Thus, the LORD saved Hezekiah and the inhabitants of Jerusalem from the

hand of Sennacherib the king of Assyria, and from the hand of all other, and guided them on every side" (2 Chronicles 32:21-22).

"Then the angel of the LORD went forth, and smote in the camp of the Assyrians a hundred and fourscore and five thousand: and when they arose early in the morning, behold, they were all dead corpses" (Isaiah 37:36).

You need to be born again; for if you are winning today with the yoke of sin upon you, it does not mean that you can always win. It is only as a result of God's grace. This may be your last chance. Sin is the yoke of transgression. No matter your title, if there is any single sin reigning over you, it is the yoke of transgression. No matter how mighty you are in any field of life; you need to break the yoke of transgression upon your life. The mighty soldiers in Babylon who succeeded in conquering the whole world with the yoke of transgression upon them, once failed. The flame of fire burnt all of them and later on in life; they lost the battle.

"Then was Nebuchadnezzar full of fury, and the form of his visage was changed against Shadrach, Meshach, and Abed-nego: therefore, he spake, and commanded that they should heat the furnace one seven times more than it was wont to be heated. And he commanded the most mighty men that were in his army to bind Shadrach, Meshach, and Abed-nego, and to cast them into the burning fiery furnace. Then these men were bound in their coats, their hosen, and their hats, and their other garments, and were cast into the midst of the burning fiery furnace. Therefore, because the king's commandment was urgent, and the furnace exceeding hot, the flame of the fire slew those men that took up Shadrach, Meshach, and Abed-nego" (Daniel 3:19-22).

You may be the richest man in the world but if you are not born again, you are bound to fail. The Total Man, written by Dan Benson, talks about some people who made it in one side of life with the yoke of transgression upon them. In this book, Dan speaks concerning Aristotle Onassis. Aristotle was a self-made victim of acute nearsightedness. It was estimated that his shipping magnate was once worth a billion dollars. Onassis owned houses, villas and apartments in half a dozen cities; a luxurious Ionian Island; a priceless art collection; and the world's most lavished yacht – the 325-foot Christina, complete with luxurious bathrooms, outfitted in Sienna marble and gold-plated faucets (Benson, Jan 1, 1977).

If he had been an American, we probably would have called him the "Great American Success Story." Aristotle Onassis had climbed from being an impoverished young man with only $60 in his pocket to one of the world wealthiest business tycoons. He was rarely without beautiful and famous women around him. A bachelor until age forty, Onassis' first marriage was to the seventeen-year-old daughter of another shipping magnet. It was not long after he began a ten-year affair with opera singer, Maria Callas, by 1968, that he was wooing Jacqueline Kennedy. While Onassis' life style reflected his philosophy of life, his words echoed that what really counts these days is money. He proclaimed: "It is the people with money who are the royalty now."

In his savor for money and all it could buy; Aristotle Onassis built his entire life on a foundation that was material. He began feeling the load of the yoke of transgression in 1973 when as Time Magazine reports:

"Onassis' life changed dramatically when his son Alexander was killed in a plane crash. He aged overnight, observed a close associate. He suddenly became an old man. In business negotiations, he was uncharacteristically absent-minded, irrational and petulant."

His son's death was like a snapping jolt to a man so protected with life's pleasantries. Rumors began to circle round the world that the tycoon's health was failing; that Onassis was deluged by flash flood of guilt over his son. Perhaps, Onassis was realizing that he had been living a life desperately out of balance. Whatever was the case, in his foundation, one misplaced building block called "more money" was crumbling. As his health failed, his business acumen also failed.

Concurrently, the Arab oil prices hit the shipping Industry hard. Fortune Magazine reported that Onassis' assets plunged from an estimated one $billion to $200 million during his last year of life.

Death claimed him in March 1975. Despite his last year losses, Onassis was still a smashing success by society standards (Benson, Jan 1, 1977).

The summary of his life is that he failed to break the yoke of transgression. He was building without God. A failure is one who lives his life without breaking the yoke of transgression.

H. G. Wells achieved world fame as a writer and a historian; but he was not born again. The yoke of transgression allowed him to read and write but his last writing before death was a disappointment. He writes: "I have no peace; all life is at the end of the Tether" (Katen, 2013).

Ralph Barton was his nation's foremost cartoonist. He left this note as he took his life; "I have had few difficulties; many friends; great successes; I have gone from wife to wife and from house to house; visited great countries of the world; but I am fed up with inventing devices to fill up twenty-four hours of the day" (Martin, 2001).

No matter your success, nobody can succeed with the yoke of transgression upon his life. All of these men were at or near the top of their chosen professions. They knew no lack of money, reputation or power. A failure is one who lives life out of balance placing undue emphasis on one or two facets of life. The yoke of transgression is the yoke of all yokes.

Job was able to succeed because he broke the yoke of transgression upon his life. Paul succeeded because he broke the yoke of transgression on his way to Damascus. Enoch succeeded because he broke the yoke of transgression.

"And Jared lived an hundred sixty and two years, and he begat Enoch: And Jared lived after he begat Enoch eight hundred years, and begat sons and daughters: And all the days of Jared were nine hundred sixty and two years: and he died. And Enoch lived sixty and five years, and begat Methuselah: And Enoch walked with God after he begat Methuselah three hundred years, and begat sons and daughters: And all the days of Enoch were three hundred sixty and five years: And Enoch

walked with God: and he was not; for God took him"
(Genesis 5:18-24).

Joseph succeeded because he broke the yoke of transgression. Jacob succeeded because he wrestled with the Lord until he broke the yoke of transgression and his name was changed.

"And Jacob was left alone; and there wrestled a man with him until the breaking of the day. And when he saw that he prevailed not against him, he touched the hollow of his thigh; and the hollow of Jacob's thigh was out of joint, as he wrestled with him. And he said, let me go, for the day breaketh. And he said, I will not let thee go, except thou bless me. And he said unto him, what is thy name? And he said, Jacob. And he said, thy name shall be called no more Jacob, but Israel: for as a prince hast thou power with God and with men, and hast prevailed" (Genesis 32:24-28).

You can succeed today if you so wish. The Lord is ready to break the yoke of transgression upon you (See Lamentations 1:14).

CHAPTER 4

THE YOKE OF THE YOUTH

Youth is the time of life when one is young. It is the period between childhood and maturity. It is the early period of existence, growth or development. It is a time between adolescence and maturity.

Anything evil that therefore takes place during the time of youth is very dangerous. When someone is placed under a yoke and that yoke is not broken, it will destroy that person.

There are general problems that befall every youth. It is natural but when it is a destructive yoke, such youth is in serious trouble. The yoke Jeremiah talked about in *Lamentations 3:27* is a normal yoke that every child who is growing should pass through. But when it is delayed; it is not the best.

On the other hand; when a destructive yoke is placed upon a youth or is born with a child; it is dangerous. There are examples of youths who suffered from yokes at early age. The brother of Abel started attacking him from his early age. Without any knowledge of the activities of household wickedness, Cain deceived Abel. He innocently followed his elder brother; who later killed him in the wilderness. It was the yoke of the youth. Abel died prematurely under a youthful yoke of household wickedness. He was not mature enough to detect the evil plan of his only brother.

When a youth is under a youthful yoke, he takes anybody as a friend. When a child is under a yoke; he may not listen to the good advice of his parents. He may go into sin with the conviction that it is the best thing to do; but will later find out to his regret that he was under a yoke. The entire first born of Egypt were under the youthful yoke of sin that destroyed their parents and they were not spared during divine judgment in Egypt. Nadab and Abihu died in the altar of God for bringing strange fire into the altar of God.

"And Nadab and Abihu, the sons of Aaron, took either of them his censer, and put fire therein, and put incense thereon, and offered strange fire before the LORD, which he commanded them not. And there went out fire from the LORD, and devoured them, and they died before the LORD" (Leviticus 10:1-2).

Any youth who is committing any sinful act in life is under youthful yoke. Cozbi and Zimri who started as boyfriend and girlfriend died under youthful yoke.

"And, behold, one of the children of Israel came and brought unto his brethren a Midianitish woman in the sight of Moses, and in the sight of all the congregation of the children of Israel, who were weeping before the door of the tabernacle of the congregation. And when Phinehas, the son of Eleazar, the son of Aaron the priest,

saw it, he rose up from among the congregation, and took a javelin in his hand; And he went after the man of Israel into the tent, and thrust both of them through, the man of Israel, and the woman through her belly. So, the plague was stayed from the children of Israel. And those that died in the plague were twenty and four thousand. And the LORD spake unto Moses, saying, Phinehas, the son of Eleazar, the son of Aaron the priest, hath turned my wrath away from the children of Israel, while he was zealous for my sake among them, that I consumed not the children of Israel in my jealousy. Wherefore say, Behold, I give unto him my covenant of peace: And he shall have it, and his seed after him, even the covenant of an everlasting priesthood; because he was zealous for his God, and made an atonement for the children of Israel. Now the name of the Israelite that was slain, even that was slain with the Midianitish woman, was Zimri, the son of Salu, a prince of a chief house among the Simeonites. And the name of the Midianitish woman that was slain was Cozbi, the daughter of Zur; he was head over a people, and of a chief house in Midian. And the LORD spake unto Moses, saying, Vex the Midianites, and smite them: For they vex you with their wiles, wherewith they have beguiled you in the matter of Peor, and in the matter of Cozbi, the daughter of a prince of Midian, their sister, which was slain in the day of the plague for Peor's sake" (Numbers 25:6-18).

When a person is under youthful yoke, he will reject every good advice. He will be restless. He will see death and run into it. He will not heed parental counsel. Absalom died under a youthful yoke; he refused to listen to advice because he felt that he could do better than the adults.

An example of a child who is under youthful yoke is one that does not have patience. They cannot read their books; go to church; pray very well, and prepare before marriage. They want to have carnal knowledge before marriage. All these are the things that destroyed Absalom (See 2 Samuel 18:9, 18). Some children die young because they have parents who put evil yoke upon them (See 1 Kings 3:16, 28). The young prophets of the bible died under youthful yoke. When a child begins to eat anyhow and listens to the enemy instead of God, he is under a youthful yoke (See 1 Kings 13:11, 32).

Jeroboam placed a yoke of the youth upon all his children by means of his sinful life. When little children begin to die in a mysterious way in some families it means there is youthful yoke.

"And it came to pass, when he reigned, that he smote all the house of Jeroboam; he left not to Jeroboam any that breathed, until he had destroyed him, according unto the saying of the LORD, which he spake by his servant Ahijah the Shilonite" (1 Kings 15:29).

The family of Baasha was destroyed because a youthful yoke was discovered in that family. When a man sins and his children inherit such sin; they are under a youthful yoke. Such yokes can wipe away a whole family. When parent's sin and the children copy it; it can bring youthful yoke that can destroy the family.

"And also by the hand of the prophet Jehu the son of Hanani came the word of the LORD against Baasha, and against his house, even for all the evil that he did in the sight of the LORD, in provoking him to anger with the work of his hands, in being like the house of Jeroboam; and because he killed him. In the twenty and sixth year of Asa king of Judah began Elah the son of Baasha to reign over Israel in Tirzah, two years. And his servant Zimri, captain of half his chariots, conspired against him, as he was in Tirzah, drinking himself drunk in the house of Arza steward of his house in Tirzah. And Zimri went in and smote him, and killed him, in the twenty and seventh year of Asa king of Judah, and reigned in his stead. And it came to pass, when he began to reign, as soon as he sat on his throne, that he slew all the house of Baasha: he left him not one that pisseth against a wall, neither of his kinsfolks, nor of his friends. Thus did Zimri destroy all the house of Baasha, according to the word of the LORD, which he spake against Baasha by Jehu the prophet, For all the sins of Baasha, and the sins of Elah his son, by which they sinned, and by which they made Israel to sin, in

provoking the LORD God of Israel to anger with their vanities. Now the rest of the acts of Elah, and all that he did, are they not written in the book of the chronicles of the kings of Israel?" (1 Kings 16:7-14).

When little children refuse to repent and begin to mock the people of God, they are under a youthful yoke that can kill them.

"And he went up from thence unto Beth–el: and as he was going up by the way, there came forth little children out of the city, and mocked him, and said unto him, go up, thou bald head; go up, thou bald head. And he turned back, and looked on them, and cursed them in the name of the LORD. And there came forth two she bears out of the wood, and tare forty and two children of them" (2 Kings 2:23-24).

When some parents are under the control of witchcraft, they can be used to place a youthful yoke upon their children and it can bring untimely death.

"And when Athaliah the mother of Ahaziah saw that her son was dead, she arose and destroyed all the seed royal" (2 Kings 11:1).

The King of Judah, Josiah, died prematurely in the hands of his enemies.

"In his days Pharaoh–nechoh king of Egypt went up against the king of Assyria to the river Euphrates: and king Josiah went against him; and he slew him at Megiddo, when he had seen him. And his servants carried him in a chariot dead from Megiddo, and brought him to Jerusalem, and buried him in his own sepulchre. And the people of the land took Jehoahaz the son of Josiah, and anointed him, and made him king in his father's stead" (2 Kings 23:29, 30).

The sons of Zedekiah were killed in the presence of their father because the yoke of the youth was upon them.

They were on the side of their father instead of taking sides with God.

> *"And it came to pass in the ninth year of his reign, in the tenth month, in the tenth day of the month, that Nebuchadnezzar king of Babylon came, he, and all his host, against Jerusalem, and pitched against it; and they built forts against it round about… And the king of Babylon smote them, and slew them at Riblah in the land of Hamath. So, Judah was carried away out of their land"* (2 Kings 25:1, 21).

The decree of an evil king can bring a yoke upon little children; and if their parents fail to hide them from such evil yoke, like the parent of Moses and Jesus, the yoke will destroy those children.

> *"Then Herod, when he saw that he was mocked of the wise men, was exceeding wroth, and sent forth, and slew all the children that were in Bethlehem, and in all the coasts thereof, from two years old and under,*

according to the time which he had diligently enquired of the wise men. Then was fulfilled that which was spoken by Jeremy the prophet, saying, In Rama was there a voice heard, lamentation, and weeping, and great mourning, Rachel weeping for her children, and would not be comforted, because they are not" *(Matthew 2:16-18).*

A youth who runs to Jesus will not suffer from evil yokes. Youths who obey God will not suffer from evil yokes. By the grace of God, many people destroyed their yoke and made it in life. Any problem that starts from childhood is an evil yoke. Any ugly trait or character that manifests in the early stages of life would be an evil yoke of the youth. Any problem that strikes when life is about to develop is a yoke of the youth. Any problem or hindrance that strikes at the beginning of any good venture is the yoke of the youth. Any power that attacks people or any establishment between birth and maturity is the yoke of the youth. All the powers fighting the growth of any good thing is the yoke of the youth. Any sickness or disease fighting against the development of any part of your organs is the yoke of the youth. Any power that is assigned to terminate any good project, vision or ministry is the yoke of the youth. The spirit of abortion and miscarriage are all classified as the yoke of the youth. Any power in the brain, which steals useful information, is also classified as the yoke of the youth. Any power that starts evil work early in people's lives is also the yoke of the youth. Any power that influences people to do things before the right time is also the yoke of the youth. A man and woman that are not married properly, yet meeting as husband and wife are under the bondage of the yoke of the youth. Doing things at the wrong time or under age especially evil things is the yoke of the youth.

"To everything there is a season, and a time to every purpose under the heaven: A time to be born, and a time to die; a time to plant, and a time to pluck up that which is planted; A time to kill, and a time to heal; a time to break down, and a time to build up; A time to weep, and a time to laugh; a time to mourn, and a time to dance; A time to cast away stones, and a time to gather stones together; a time to embrace, and a time to refrain from

embracing; A time to get, and a time to lose; a time to keep, and a time to cast away; A time to rend, and a time to sew; a time to keep silence, and a time to speak; A time to love, and a time to hate; a time of war, and a time of peace" (Ecclesiastes 3:1-8).

Jesus is the only person who can break the yoke of the youth and set the youths free. He loves children (the youth) and cares for them very well. Even death cannot stand the rebuke of Jesus. Jesus can follow any youth who invites him into their life and break their yokes. The parents in the past who invited Jesus into the situations of their children did not regret it.

"While he spake these things unto them, behold, there came a certain ruler, and worshipped him, saying, my daughter is even now dead: but come and lay thy hand upon her, and she shall live. And Jesus arose, and followed him, and so did his disciples... And when Jesus came into the ruler's house, and saw the minstrels and

the people making a noise… And the fame hereof went abroad into all that land" (Matthew 9:18-19, 23, 26).

The yokes of the youths are broken at the presence of Jesus. When the yoke of the youth attacked the only son of his parents unto death, Jesus intervened.

"And it came to pass the day after, that he went into a city called Nain; and many of his disciples went with him, and much people. Now when he came nigh to the gate of the city, behold, there was a dead man carried out, the only son of his mother, and she was a widow: and much people of the city was with her. And when the Lord saw her, he had compassion on her, and said unto her, Weep not. And he came and touched the bier: and they that bare him stood still. And he said, Young man, I say unto thee, Arise. And he that was dead sat up, and began to speak. And he delivered him to his mother" (Luke 7:11-15).

There was a man whose yoke started working against his life from the very point of conception to the day of his birth. The same yoke followed him after he was born for forty good years. That is the yoke of the youth. It is a problem that grows up with people that is called the yoke of the youth. No matter how old you are now, the problem that you grew up with and still see in your life is the yoke of your youth. It could be sickness; it could be poverty. It could be pains. It could be hatred. It could also be a particular sin, which you started fighting from childhood and even now still comes from time to time.

"And as Jesus passed by, he saw a man which was blind from his birth. And his disciples asked him, saying, Master, who did sin, this man, or his parents, that he was born blind? Jesus answered, neither hath this man sinned, nor his parents: but that the works of God should be made manifest in him" (John 9:1-3).

Yours may have started before you were born or after you were born. Maybe you grew up and found it out. It is the yoke of the youth. Jesus is out looking for such problems in order to destroy them. Present yourself to Him and your problem would be over.

> *"When he had thus spoken, he spat on the ground, and made clay of the spittle, and he anointed the eyes of the blind man with the clay, and said unto him, Go, wash in the pool of Siloam, (which is by interpretation, Sent.) He went his way therefore, and washed, and came seeing" (John 9:6-7).*

From today, the Lord will break the yoke of your youth and set you free, in the name of Jesus. Amen!

CHAPTER 5

THE YOKE OF THE JAW

According to Wikipedia, The jaw is any opposable articulated structure at the entrance of the mouth, typically used for grasping and manipulating food. The term jaw is also broadly applied to the whole of the structures constituting the vault of the mouth and serving to open and close it and is part of the body plan of most animals. A jaw is either of two complex cartilaginous or bony structures in most vertebrates that border the mouth supporting the soft-parts enclosing it. In its verb usage, it can also mean to talk incessantly and tiresomely;

to talk abusively; indignantly or long-windedly. It means to talk to somebody in a scolding or boring manner.

The yoke of the Jaw makes its victims to open their mouth at the wrong time and close it when it is supposed to be open. This yoke causes her victims to talk indignantly against its helpers. When someone is yoked with a jaw yoke; such a person scolds everyone without consideration.

"I drew them with cords of a man, with bands of love: and 1 was to them as they that take off the yoke on their jaws, and I laid meat unto them" (Hosea 11:4).

Satan puts on all the dumb people in the past and of the present generation this yoke. It serves two main purposes: to keep the mouth completely out of talking or to cause people to talk wrongly.

We are going to discuss them one after the other to see what jaw yokes have done.

JAW YOKE UPON THE DUMB

When some people get yoked with jaw yokes, they either get deaf and dumb or they go to the other extreme. In the bible days, this yoke dealt with some people also.

> *"And at even, when the sun did set, they brought unto him all that were diseased, and them that were possessed with devils... And in the morning, rising up a great while before day, he went out, and departed into a solitary place, and there prayed"* (Mark 1:32, 35).

The yoke of the jaw opened the mouth of many people in Israel and made them to become drunkards. Any power that can open your mouth to say any wrong thing or do any wrong thing is the yoke of the jaw. Any power that can also close your mouths and prevent you from saying all that you are supposed to say is the yoke of the jaw. People that are spiritually yoked with the yoke of the jaw together with their businesses and careers can never make any meaningful spiritual progress (See Psalms 38:13).

"Their poison is like the poison of a serpent: they are like the deaf adder that stoppeth her ear" (Psalms 58:4).

This yokes also make people stubborn. When they hear the word of God; they will not obey it. This is the yoke that makes people to hear the word of God clearly; but they will never do it. Adam and Eve knew the fruit that was forbidden to be eaten; but Satan placed the yoke of the jaw upon them; and they became like the deaf adder that stops her ear. Cain knew that God hates murderers but he closed his ears and killed his only brother.

Someone under the bondage of the yoke of the jaw can decide not to obey God. This was the yoke Satan used against Moses when he began to give reasons to God.

"And Moses said unto the LORD, O my Lord, I am not eloquent, neither heretofore, nor since thou hast spoken unto thy servant: but I am slow of speech, and of a slow tongue. And the LORD said unto him, who hath made man's mouth? Or who maketh the dumb, or deaf, or the

seeing, or the blind? Have not I the LORD?" (Exodus 4:10-11).

This was the yoke that made Pharaoh to clearly hear the word of God but because he was under this yoke, he challenged God. God told the children of Israel to rest on the Sabbath day but because some of them were victims of this yoke, they left their houses on the Sabbath to gather manner.

"And it came to pass, that there went out some of the people on the seventh day for to gather, and they found none... And the house of Israel called the name thereof Manna: and it was like coriander seed, white; and the taste of it was like wafers made with honey" (Exodus 16:27, 31).

The yoke of the jaw makes people rebellious and stubborn. This was the yoke that prevailed over Aaron and he made an image for the children of Israel to worship. This was the yoke that manipulated the lives of

Korah, Dathan and Abiran and they started talking nonsense against Moses. That was why God buried them alive and used fire against the remaining ones.

> *"Now Korah, the son of Izhar, the son of Kohath, the son of Levi, and Dathan and Abiram, the sons of Eliab, and On, the son of Peleth, sons of Reuben, took men… But if the LORD make a new thing, and the earth open her mouth, and swallow them up, with all that appertain unto them, and they go down quick into the pit; then ye shall understand that these men have provoked the LORD" (Numbers 16:1, 30).*

This was the yoke that made all the congregation of Israel to open their mouths and murmured against Moses and Aaron and also accused them of murder. As a result of this yoke, fourteen thousand seven hundred of them died immediately.

> *"But on the morrow, all the congregation of the children of Israel murmured against Moses and against Aaron,*

By Prayer M. Madueke

saying, Ye have killed the people of the LORD… And Aaron returned unto Moses unto the door of the tabernacle of the congregation: and the plague was stayed" (Numbers 16:41, 50).

When this yoke fell upon Gehazi, the servant of Elisha, he told a blatant lie against God and the man of God. This yoke closed the heart and the mouth of Gehazi from repentance.

When this yoke came upon Jezebel, the wife of Ahab, she threatened Elijah's life, killed Naboth and took his vineyard; aiding her husband, Ahab, to sin against God.

"And it came to pass after these things, that Naboth the Jezreelite had a vineyard, which was in Jezreel, hard by the palace of Ahab king of Samaria… And thou shalt speak unto him, saying, thus saith the LORD, Hast thou killed, and also taken possession? And thou shalt speak unto him, saying, thus saith the LORD, In the place where dogs licked the blood of Naboth shall dogs lick thy blood, even thine" (1 Kings 21:1, 19)·

Finally, she was killed and she died under this yoke. Dogs feasted on her flesh and blood (2 Kings 9:30, 37).

This was the yoke that yoked the jaw of Sennacherib and he opened his mouth against God. He limited and really blasphemed the name of the Living God; and when he got home that evening, he met war in his house; and his army barracks was invaded. He also died together with one hundred and seventy-five thousand soldiers (See *2 Chronicles 32, 11:9-20; 2 Kings 18:9-35, 19:1-71, 19:37, 2 Chronicles 32:21).*

This yoke brought the whole people in Assyria under subjection and they opened their mouths and boasted against God (See Isaiah 10:5-19).

When this yoke came upon the jaws of the nation of Moab, they were filled with pride and became liars that God responded and said that the people of Moab shall howl, mourn, etc. (See Isaiah 16:6, 63).

"The yoke of the jaw opened the mouth of many people in Israel and made them to become drunkards. Any power that can open your mouth to say any wrong thing or do any wrong thing is the yoke of the jaw. Any power that can also close your mouth and prevent you from saying all that you are supposed to say is the yoke of the jaw. Many people's lives, careers, businesses, marriages and destinies have been wasted because of unsaid words or over-said words" (Joel 1:5).

The yoke of the jaw can do much harm to the victim. It is one of the yokes that Satan and occult people have used to control great men and women of all generation. An old illiterate in the village of an agent of Satan anywhere can use this yoke to control a whole community or even an institution. It can be used to force people to say things according to their wish. An occultist can manipulate the voice of a whole city, to voice out words to his favor. It can equally be used against learned chief judge or magistrate to pervert judgment. They can talk through victims without the victim's knowledge.

"For in many things we offend all. If any man offend not in word, the same is a perfect man, and able also to bridle the whole body" (James 3:2).

They cause their victims to use offensive word through the yoke of the jaw by opening their victim's mouth. You may not be able to control your speech, if they are manipulating your words with the yoke of jaws. The yoke of jaw is an occult yoke, used all over African and the entire world to pass evil decrees, evil judgments or verdicts. It can be used against the members of the Legislature to pass evil laws that can affect the whole nations. It was used in America to forbid Bible and prayers in public schools. It was also used to legalize abortion in many nations of the world. Such laws affect a whole nation and it is an insult to the church and the entire nation. African leaders especially, are using this yoke to manipulate the lawmakers. The yoke of the jaw is a witchcraft yoke to make people say what is wrong and to close peoples' mouth from saying what is right. It makes people to say the right things, when it is too late, and make people to demand evil from their fellow human beings.

It can be used to control your hand or leg during driving. It can be used to control any part of your body: eyes to focus on evil; mind to think on evil; hands to touch evil fruits in the Garden of Eden. It can be used to manipulate any part of your organ to commit sin. The yoke of the jaw can be used to bridle some parts of your body or the whole body.

As it could be used against a horse to obey, it could also be used against a human being to obey.

> *"Behold, we put bits in the horses' mouths, that they may obey us; and we turn about their whole body. Behold also the ships, which though they be so great, and are driven of fierce winds, yet are they turned about with a very small helm, whithersoever the governor listeth. Even so the tongue is a little member, and boasteth great things. Behold, how great a matter a little fire kindleth! And the tongue is a fire, a world of iniquity: so is the tongue among our members, that it*

defileth the whole body, and setteth on fire the course of nature; and it is set on fire of hell" (James 3:3-6).

Whoever allows the yoke of the jaw to open his or her mouth will speak boastfully or wrongly. The enemy used the victims of jaw-yoked people to speak great things and to kindle evil fires of iniquities. It can be used to defile a whole congregation; and set on fire the course of nature, which will finally take people to hell fire.

The devil has used mankind in the evil society to do great evil. They can use the yoke of jaws to keep a professor who is very vocal, quiet. They can use it to close the mouth of a great politician. They can use the yoke of the jaws to control a man who is operating like a beast of the field or the man flying everywhere like the witchcraft bird or the great wise serpent moving around the wilderness. You can be as wise as serpent and as harmless as a dove; simple as children; compassionate as the savior; strong in faith, not staggering at the promise of God. Whoever you are; if you allow the occult or evil priests to place a yoke of the jaw upon you, they will stop you from acting according to divine ways.

"For every kind of beasts, and of birds, and of serpents, and of things in the sea, is tamed, and hath been tamed of mankind" (James 3:7).

If you claim to be a Christian (or whoever you are) and you allow your tongue to be under the control of Satan, you are under the yoke of the jaw. If your tongue speaks unruly, evil things and brings out poisonous words, you are under the yoke of the jaw. Even though you preach as a Pastor and miracles still happens; even if you can raise the dead but your tongue is untamed by God through his written Word, you are under the yoke of the jaw.

If you use your tongue to bless God and eventually use the same tongue to curse men, who are made in the similitude of the Lord, you are under the yoke of the jaw. If God alone is not the controller of your tongue and life, you are under the bondage of the yoke of the jaw.

"But the tongue can no man tame; it is an unruly evil, full of deadly poison... Can the fig tree, my brethren,

bear olive berries? Either a vine, figs? So can no fountain both yield salt water and fresh" (James 3:8, 12).

Whosoever claims to be a Christian or a minister, who will leave this world at trumpet sound, in a twinkle of an eye, whosoever says that he is wise should show it by using his tongue to the glory of God. Let his conversation and his works be done with meekness unto wisdom.

No matter your reason, if you have bitterness, envy, devilish wisdom, and strife in your heart, you are under the bondage of the yoke of the jaws.

"Who is a wise man and endued with knowledge among you? Let him shew out of a good conversation his works with meekness of wisdom" (James 3:13).

This yoke of the jaws opened the mouth of Herod to ask the daughter of Herodias to "ask for anything she wanted, even if it meant half of his kingdom. The same yoke of the jaw made Herod to swear unto her,

"Whatsoever thou shalt ask of me I will give it thee, unto the half of my kingdom" (See Mark 6:22).

The same yoke of the jaw opened the mouth of the daughter of Herodias to ask her mother, "What shall I ask?" The same yoke opened the mouth to Herodias' wife and she said "the head of John the Baptist." The same yoke also opened the mouth of the daughter of Herodias and she asked again saying, "l will that thou give me by and by in a charger the head of John the Baptist."

"And king Herod heard of him; (for his name was spread abroad:) and he said, That John the Baptist was risen from the dead, and therefore mighty works do shew forth themselves in him... And she came in straightway with haste unto the king, and asked, saying, I will that thou give me by and by in a charger the head of John the Baptist" (Mark 6:14, 25).

The same yoke of the jaw immediately sent an executioner and commanded his head to be brought and he went and beheaded him in the prison. The small-possessed daughter of Herodias received the head of our great John the Baptist in a charger as Herod's birthday gift. She handed it over to her mother, the great adulterer.

"And the king was exceeding sorry; yet for his oath's sake, and for their sakes, which sat with him, he would not reject her. And immediately the king sent an executioner, and commanded his head to be brought: and he went and beheaded him in the prison, and brought his head in a charger, and gave it to the damsel: and the damsel gave it to her mother" (Mark 6:26-28).

It is the same yoke of the jaws that opened the mouth of Herod, the mouth of the daughter of Herodias and the mouth of the Herodias' wife, and closed the mouth of John the Baptist. The occult and witchcraft of John's days that were once afraid of John the Baptist bewitched John with the yoke of the jaw.

"For Herod feared John, knowing that he was a just man and an holy, and observed him; and when he heard him,

he did many things, and heard him gladly" (Mark 6:20).

The yoke of jaws closed the mouth of John the Baptist and he submitted his head to the executioners and his head was used to celebrate the birthday of a sinner. The birthday of Herod, the wicked, was celebrated with the head of John the Baptist in a charger.

John the Baptist died and was buried but his disciples did not bury his head because it was used as a birthday gift.

"And when his disciples heard of it, they came and took up his corpse, and laid it in a tomb" (Mark 6:29).

WHO WAS JOHN THE BAPTIST?

Who was John the Baptist? John the Baptist was the son of Zachariah of the course of Abia. John the Baptist was the son of Elizabeth the wife of Zachariah, the priest of the Lord. John the Baptist was a prophet. The angel of God announced his conception and birth. He was a man whose birth brought joy and gladness into the lives of many. He was a man, great in the sight of the Lord. He was not to drink wine or any strong drink and yet he was filled and always intoxicated by the Holy Ghost from his mother's womb. Many people turned to the Lord their God through his ministry. He came out from his mother's womb and went into the world with the spirit and the power of Elijah, to turn the hearts of the fathers to the children and the disobedient to the wisdom of the just. He was born and filled in the Holy Ghost from the womb, to make ready a people prepared for the Lord.

"There was in the days of Herod, the king of Judæa, a certain priest named Zacharias, of the course of Abia: and his wife was of the daughters of Aaron, and her name was Elisabeth… And he shall go before him in the

spirit and power of Elias, to turn the hearts of the fathers to the children, and the disobedient to the wisdom of the just; to make ready a people prepared for the Lord" *(Luke 1:5, 17).*

I am more concerned about John the Baptist, and more about what God said he would do.

He was born with the Spirit of Elijah; the Spirit that God invested upon Elijah. That means that he should pattern his life like Elijah and leave the world the same way Elijah left the world.

WHAT DID GOD DO WITH THE SPIRIT OF ELIJAH?

- Elijah was the only prophet in his generation that opposed and defeated Ahab perfectly (See 1 Kings 18).

- He boldly opposed the government of Ahab with the word and prophecies of God.

- He survived the destructive famine in Israel and God used his ministry to sustain a widow and her son (See 1 Kings 17:8, 16).

- He boldly appeared before his greatest enemy who was looking for him everywhere to destroy his life (See 1 Kings 18:1-4, 7, 39).

- He challenged alone all the prophets of Baal and prayed fire down to confirm the true God (See 1 Kings 18:7, 39).

- He fearlessly put before Ahab his sins and declared God's judgment upon his family (See 1 Kings 21:15-24).

- He trained Elisha and handed him his anointing in a double way (See 2 Kings 2:1-15).

- He closed heaven and there was no rain or dew for three years and six months (See 1 Kings 1:17).

- He prayed and opened the heaven after 3 years and six months (See l Kings 1:8).

- He raised a dead child; the son of a woman (See l King 17:17-14)

- He received strength to fast for 40 days and 40 nights (See l Kings 19:8).

He was the only prophet in his generation and other generations that refused to die. He went home alive. He was taken to heaven by a chariot of fire and horses of fire and went up by a whirlwind into Heaven. As he was going, he dropped his mantle to Elisha who took after him (See 1 Kings 2:12).

In my own understanding, John the Baptist was not supposed to die. He had the same Spirit of Elijah, which is the Spirit of fire. He started very well, but to me, he did not end well. He challenged Herod and his wife; who both had the spirit of Ahab and Jezebel. But he did not resist the attacks of Herod and his family, like Elijah did to the attacks of Ahab and Jezebel. John the Baptist didn't put up any challenge to his death. He submitted to death, whereas Elijah fought and rejected death with the same Spirit. He was supposed to go with the chariot of fire; with whirlwind; but he died in the hand of a sinner. Elijah overcame the witchcraft of Ahab and Jezebel but John the Baptist was a victim of the yoke of the jaw. If you don't say what you are supposed to say, you may die before your time. You may die while your mother and father are still alive. You may allow the occult people in your family to use your head as a birthday gift. You may be the source of the prosperity to the occult people around you. Don't give your jaws to the yoke of the jaw. Don't die before your time.

"Submit yourselves therefore to God. Resist the devil, and he will flee from you" (James 4:7).

Elijah did something that John the Baptist could not do. He was a man of fire, but he never used the fire at the time of need. He could have commanded fire to burn both Herod and his wife. He could have commanded fire to burn both the executioners and the daughter of the Herodias. But he was too 'holy' and ignorant of Holy Ghost fire. His holiness had water and fire but he used only water in his baptism. He failed to use the fire when he needed it most. God is a merciful God and also a consuming fire.

Are you Elijah or John the Baptist? Do you know when to pray fire prayers with judgment, and when to pray water prayer and mercy? How is your prayer life? Can your prayer touch your Ahab, Jezebel and their prophets? Do your prayers pity your Ahab, Jezebel and the family of Herod? How are your prayers like, is it balanced or in the extreme?

If you don't know how to pray against your Herod, his wife and their daughters, pray that you will not die before them. Don't die when you are supposed to be alive. Don't let your enemies attend your burial ceremony. The yoke of the jaw keeps people's mouth shut and opens them wide for evil utterances. When a witch or a wizard opens his mouth against your marriage, business, destiny, etc., you are in trouble. Learn how to send evil words back to the senders. Moses did it and it worked for him.

"And Moses was very wroth, and said unto the LORD, Respect not thou their offering: I have not taken one ass from them, neither have I hurt one of them… And there came out a fire from the LORD, and consumed the two hundred and fifty men that offered incense" (Numbers 16:15, 35).

Esther and Mordecai did it and it worked for them (See Esther 4:13-9, 9:13)

It is better for Achan to die than for Ai to wipe away a whole nation. It is better for Cain to die than Abel. If somebody must die, it must not be you. It is better for Saul to die than David. It is better for the prophets of Baal to die than Elijah. If anybody must die; unless he has completed his God-given ministry, like Stephen, a Christian should not die prematurely. If anybody must fail in business, exams or marriage, it must not be a Christian.

But if it is the will of God for the wicked, the witches and wizard to be born again and they are willing, let them be assisted. Jonah should not be angry because God wanted to save the wicked witches and wizards of Nineveh. If all the witches and wizards are willing to repent and forsake their sins, let us do everything to assist them.

But instead of Daniel to die in the lion's den, let Daniel's enemies be eaten up by lions.

"And the king commanded, and they brought those men which had accused Daniel, and they cast them into the den of lions, them, their children, and their wives; and the lions had the mastery of them, and brake all their bones in pieces or ever they came at the bottom of the den. Then king Darius wrote unto all people, nations, and languages, that dwell in all the earth; Peace be multiplied unto you. I make a decree, that in every dominion of my kingdom men tremble and fear before the God of Daniel: for he is the living God, and steadfast forever, and his kingdom that which shall not be destroyed, and his dominion shall be even unto the end. He delivereth and rescueth, and he worketh signs and wonders in heaven and in earth, who hath delivered Daniel from the power of the lions. So, this Daniel

prospered in the reign of Darius, and in the reign of Cyrus the Persian" (Daniel 6:24-28).

True believers should live to discern the signs of the hour. We must be sensible and sensitive to the Spirit. We must know the time of action to each purpose upon the earth. Hannah said that "The Lord killeth, and maketh alive: he bringeth down to the grave, and bringeth up" (See 1 Samuel 2:6). No matter how many times you pray and shout die, die, die; nobody will die and nothing will die if is not the time of death allowed by God. If John died, it is because God allowed it to teach us lessons. We must discern and be sensitive to the voice of the hour.

"To everything there is a season, and a time to every purpose under the heaven: A time to be born, and a time to die; a time to plant, and a time to pluck up that which is planted; A time to kill, and a time to heal; a time to break down, and a time to build up; 4A time to weep, and a time to laugh; a time to mourn, and a time to dance; A time to cast away stones, and a time to gather

stones together; a time to embrace, and a time to refrain from embracing; A time to get, and a time to lose; a time to keep, and a time to cast away; A time to rend, and a time to sew; a time to keep silence, and a time to speak; A time to love, and a time to hate; a time of war, and a time of peace" (Ecclesiastes 3:1-8).

You can take your decision. You can break the yoke of the jaw against your destiny. You must speak out when you are supposed to speak out. Do not allow the executioners of your days to cut short your life.

CHAPTER 6

YOKE OF BONDAGE

This is the yoke that can hold a person or group of persons in a specific bondage.

"Stand fast therefore in the liberty wherewith Christ hath made us free, and be not entangled again with the yoke of bondage" (Galatians 5:1).

This is the yoke that makes its victims foolish. It does not allow people to take a firm decision. It is a yoke that hates a firm decision. It is a yoke that makes her victims to live an inconsistent and unsteady life. It is a yoke of "Yes Sir!" to every Dick and Harry. Yokes of bondage keep people arrested to a peculiar problem or sin. Her victim may hear the word of God, cry and promise never to go back into sin, only to go back to it the next moment. It is a yoke of besetting sin.

> "Wherefore seeing we also are compassed about with so great a cloud of witnesses, let us lay aside every weight, and the sin which doth so easily beset us, and let us run with patience the race that is set before us" (Hebrew 12:1).

I came across a young lady in her final year in one of the universities in Africa. She passed through our deliverance session and in one of the days of the program her problem was mentioned. After the deliverance prayers, she confessed to me that she had been in bondage for many years. She was married with four children. From the time she got married, she had been sleeping with her husband's younger brother, in the same compound.

Because her husband was in a permanent night business, they used the opportunity to sleep together in sin. They could not do without each other. They went to the same university, read the same course, studied together, and slept in the same bed almost every night. Her relationship had caused a lot of problems. A concerned friend brought her to the church. The Lord immediately pointed to her immoral acts. She came to me and gave me the details of their relationship. It was a serious abomination.

So many things are going on under the sun. Only God can tell what the evil men have done in this world. After the message that Sunday morning, she cried, repented and took a firm decision to terminate the relationship. She left the church with that strong decision, but before she knew what she was doing, the power of sin had pushed her into the boy's room and the immorality took place again. She kept repenting and falling into the same sin until I was transferred from that town. That was a yoke of bondage.

WHAT IS BONDAGE?

Bondage is the state of being under the control of another person. It is the state of being under the control of a force or influence or abstract power.

Bondage is a state of being bound by compulsion. Bondage is captivity. Bondage involves servitude or subjugation to a controlling person or force.

When a young man yokes a woman with the yoke of bondage into immorality, she will live her life to serve the man as a slave. It is also the same in every other area of life. To be in bondage is also to be under any kind of yoke. So, we may not say much on this topic.

Bondage is a gate in itself: Any type of yoke brings one into bondage. What Paul told the Galatia Christians was to take a firm decision once and for all against sin.

We should stand at liberty where Christ has delivered us out of sin. Going back to sin means entangling yourself again with the yoke of bondage.

"Stand fast therefore in the liberty wherewith Christ hath made us free, and be not entangled again with the yoke of bondage" (Galatians 5:1).

THE YOKE OF UNBELIEF

An unbeliever is someone who does not believe with all his heart, in the saving power that is in the blood of Jesus. He is a person who says that he believes in Christ with his mouth but does not honor him.

"He that cometh from above is above all: he that is of the earth is earthly, and speaketh of the earth: he that cometh from heaven is above all. And what he hath seen and heard, that he testifieth; and no man receiveth his testimony. He that hath received his testimony hath set to his seal that God is true. For he whom God hath sent speaketh the words of God: for God giveth not the Spirit by measure unto him" (John 3:31-34).

Once you are still under the bondage of many sins you are regarded as an unbeliever.

> *"He that committeth sin is of the devil; for the devil sinneth from the beginning. For this purpose, the Son of God was manifested, that he might destroy the works of the devil. Whosoever is born of God doth not commit sin; for his seed remaineth in him: and he cannot sin, because he is born of God"* (1 John 3:8-9).

What then is the yoke of unbelief? The yoke of unbelief is the power that is keeping someone under the bondage of sin. It is the power that does not allow a person to belief in Christianity. It is the power that is against righteousness that is in Christ. It is the power that keeps people in sin unto the day of death. The yoke of unbelief is the yoke that can strike and bring a victim into sin by fire. With the yoke of unbelief, sin is compulsory.

> *"Be ye not unequally yoked together with unbelievers: for what fellowship hath righteousness with*

unrighteousness? And what communion hath light with darkness?" (2 Corinthians 6:14).

It makes people just to disbelieve God. The yoke of unbelief is a yoke that keeps people happy in sin. It is the yoke that makes people sad to righteousness. This was the yoke that provoked Cain to be unhappy every day because Abel his younger brother was at peace with God. This yoke kept him unhappy until he killed his only brother. It is the yoke that causes people to prefer wickedness than pity. It is a heartless yoke. It is the yoke of the sadist.

While the yoke of transgression causes people to transgress with regret, the yoke of unbelief causes people to rejoice in evil. This was the yoke that gave Pharaoh happiness when he saw the children of God in sorrow. It gave Pharaoh joy to see that God has nobody to serve Him. This is the yoke that causes people to blaspheme the name of the Lord.

"And the son of an Israelitish woman, whose father was an Egyptian, went out among the children of Israel: and this son of the Israelitish woman and a man of Israel strove together in the camp; And the Israelitish woman's son blasphemed the name of the LORD, and cursed. And they brought him unto Moses: (and his mother's name was Shelomith, the daughter of Dibri, of the tribe of Dan:) And they put him in ward, that the mind of the LORD might be shewed them. And the LORD spake unto Moses, saying" (Leviticus 24:10-13).

This yoke compelled the people of Amalek to hate God and His children. They smote the children of God without mercy.

"If brethren dwell together, and one of them die, and have no child, the wife of the dead shall not marry without unto a stranger: her husband's brother shall go in unto her, and take her to him to wife, and perform the duty of an husband's brother unto her… Remember

what Amalek did unto thee by the way, when ye were come forth out of Egypt; How he met thee by the way, and smote the hindmost of thee, even all that were feeble behind thee, when thou wast faint and weary; and he feared not God. Therefore it shall be, when the LORD thy God hath given thee rest from all thine enemies round about, in the land which the LORD thy God giveth thee for an inheritance to possess it, that thou shalt blot out the remembrance of Amalek from under heaven; thou shalt not forget it" (Deuteronomy 25:5, 17-19).

This is the yoke that causes people to abandon the worship of the true God and gives them joy in idolatry (See *Deuteronomy 29:12, 29).* The yoke of unbelief is the yoke that was on King Nahash, which made him extremely wicked and heartless.

"Then Nahash the Ammonite came up, and encamped against Jabesh–gilead: and all the men of Jabesh said unto Nahash, make a covenant with us, and we will

serve thee. And Nahash the Ammonite answered them, on this condition will I make a covenant with you, that I may thrust out all your right eyes, and lay it for a reproach upon all Israel. And the elders of Jabesh said unto him, give us seven days' respite, that we may send messengers unto all the coasts of Israel: and then, if there be no man to save us, we will come out to thee" (1 Samuel 11:1-3).

This yoke was upon Jezebel when she threatened to kill Elijah and made her to kill Naboth, taking his vineyard by force. This yoke made her to aid Ahab to commit sin against God (See *1 Kings 19:2, 16:29; 34; 21:5-15).*

This yoke made Athaliah to kill all the royal seed to enable her become a queen without a rival.

"And when Athaliah the mother of Ahaziah saw that her son was dead, she arose and destroyed all the seed royal" (2 Kings 11:1).

When this yoke came upon the unbelieving world, they became heartless, rude and lay in wait for blood. They began to hunt every man and his brother with net. They started doing all manner of evil.

"Woe is me! For I am as when they have gathered the summer fruits, as the grape gleanings of the vintage: there is no cluster to eat: my soul desired the first ripe fruit. The good man is perished out of the earth: and there is none upright among men: they all lie in wait for blood; they hunt every man his brother with a net. That they may do evil with both hands earnestly, the prince asketh, and the judge asketh for a reward; and the great man, he uttereth his mischievous desire: so, they wrap it up. The best of them is as a brier: the most upright is sharper than a thorn hedge: the day of thy watchmen and thy visitation cometh; now shall be their perplexity" (Micah 7:1-4).

When the unbelieving Nineveh was yoked, they were filled with lies and robbery. Their whoredoms became many, and prostitution increased with witchcraft (See Nahum 3:1-4).

This was the yoke that came upon the king of Babylon and he made an image of gold. He commanded all people to fall down and worship the image. In fury, also, he commanded his most senior army officers to bind Shedrack, Meshack and Abednego to be cast into the burning fiery furnace.

"Nebuchadnezzar the king made an image of gold, whose height was threescore cubits, and the breadth thereof six cubits: he set it up in the plain of Dura, in the province of Babylon. Then Nebuchadnezzar the king sent to gather together the princes, the governors, and the captains, the judges, the treasurers, the counselors, the sheriffs, and all the rulers of the provinces, to come to the dedication of the image which Nebuchadnezzar the king had set up. Then the princes, the governors, and captains, the judges, the treasurers, the counselors, the sheriffs, and all the rulers of the provinces, were

gathered together unto the dedication of the image that Nebuchadnezzar the king had set up; and they stood before the image that Nebuchadnezzar had set up. Then an herald cried aloud, To you it is commanded, O people, nations, and languages, That at what time ye hear the sound of the cornet, flute, harp, sackbut, psaltery, dulcimer, and all kinds of musick, ye fall down and worship the golden image that Nebuchadnezzar the king hath set up: And whoso falleth not down and worshippeth shall the same hour be cast into the midst of a burning fiery furnace. Therefore, at that time, when all the people heard the sound of the cornet, flute, harp, sackbut, psaltery, and all kinds of musick, all the people, the nations, and the languages, fell down and worshipped the golden image that Nebuchadnezzar the king had set up. Wherefore at that time certain Chaldeans came near, and accused the Jews. They spake and said to the king Nebuchadnezzar, O king, live forever. Thou, O king, hast made a decree, that every man that shall hear the sound of the cornet, flute, harp, sackbut, psaltery, and dulcimer, and all kinds of musick, shall fall down and worship the golden image: And whoso falleth not down and worshippeth, that he should be cast into the midst of a burning fiery furnace. There are certain Jews whom thou hast set over the affairs of the province of Babylon, Shadrach, Meshach, and Abed–nego; these men, O king, have not regarded thee: they serve not thy gods, nor worship the golden image which thou hast set up. Then Nebuchadnezzar in his rage and fury commanded to bring Shadrach, Meshach, and Abed–nego. Then they brought these men before the king. Nebuchadnezzar spake and said unto them, is it true, O Shadrach, Meshach, and Abed–nego, do not ye serve my gods, nor worship the golden image which I have set up? Now if ye be ready that at what time ye hear the sound of the cornet, flute, harp, sackbut, psaltery, and dulcimer, and all kinds of musick, ye fall down and worship the image which I have made; well: but if ye worship not, ye shall be cast the same hour into the midst of a burning fiery furnace; and who is that God that shall deliver you out of my hands? Shadrach, Meshach, and Abed–nego, answered and said to the king, O Nebuchadnezzar, we are not careful to answer thee in this matter. If it be so, our God whom we serve is able to deliver us from the burning fiery furnace, and he will deliver us out of thine hand, O king. But if not, be it known unto thee, O king, that we will not serve thy gods, nor worship the golden image, which thou hast set up. Then was Nebuchadnezzar full of fury, and the form of his visage was changed against Shadrach, Meshach, and Abed-nego: therefore, he spake, and commanded that they should heat the furnace one seven times more than it was wont to be heated. And he commanded the most mighty men that were in his army to bind Shadrach, Meshach, and Abed-nego, and to cast them into the burning fiery furnace. Then these men were bound in their coats, their hosen, and their hats, and their other garments, and were cast into the midst of the burning fiery furnace" (Daniel 3:1-21).

This yoke made all the colleagues of Daniel to consult together and make an evil decree against Daniel and the only true God. They all succeeded in putting Daniel into the lion's den because he was the only one among them living a holy life.

"All the presidents of the kingdom, the governors, and the princes, the counselors, and the captains, have consulted together to establish a royal statute, and to make a firm decree, that whosoever shall ask a petition of any God or man for thirty days, save of thee, O king, he shall be cast into the den of lions. Now, O king, establish the decree, and sign the writing, that it be not changed, according to the law of the Medes and Persians, which altereth not. Wherefore king Darius signed the writing and the decree. Now when Daniel knew that the writing was signed, he went into his house; and his windows being open in his chamber toward Jerusalem, he kneeled upon his knees three times a day, and prayed, and gave thanks before his God, as he did aforetime. Then these men assembled, and found Daniel praying and making supplication before his God. Then they came near, and spake before the king concerning the king's decree; Hast thou not signed a decree, that every man that shall ask a petition of any God or man within thirty days, save of thee, O king, shall be cast into the den of lions? The king answered and said, the thing is true, according to the law of the

Medes and Persians, which altereth not. Then answered they and said before the king, That Daniel, which is of the children of the captivity of Judah, regardeth not thee, O king, nor the decree that thou hast signed, but maketh his petition three times a day. Then the king, when he heard these words, was sore displeased with himself, and set his heart on Daniel to deliver him: and he labored till the going down of the sun to deliver him. Then these men assembled unto the king, and said unto the king, Know, O king, that the law of the Medes and Persians is, that no decree nor statute, which the king establisheth, may be changed. Then the king commanded, and they brought Daniel, and cast him into the den of lions. Now the king spake and said unto Daniel, Thy God whom thou servest continually, he will deliver thee. And a stone was brought, and laid upon the mouth of the den; and the king sealed it with his own signet, and with the signet of his lords; that the purpose might not be changed concerning Daniel" (Daniel 6:7-17).

This yoke also came upon Haman and he secured permission to decree against all the children of God in the whole world so that they will die in one day and their properties taken over.

"And when Haman saw that Mordecai bowed not, nor did him reverence, then was Haman full of wrath. And he thought scorn to lay hands on Mordecai alone; for they had shewed him the people of Mordecai: wherefore Haman sought to destroy all the Jews that were throughout the whole kingdom of Ahasuerus, even the people of Mordecai. In the first month, that is, the month Nisan, in the twelfth year of king Ahasuerus, they cast Pur, that is, the lot, before Haman from day to day, and from month to month, to the twelfth month, that is, the month Adar. And Haman said unto king Ahasuerus, there is a certain people scattered abroad and dispersed among the people in all the provinces of thy kingdom; and their laws are diverse from all people; neither keep they the king's laws: therefore, it is not for the king's profit to suffer them. If it please the king, let it be written that they may be destroyed: and I will pay

ten thousand talents of silver to the hands of those that have the charge of the business, to bring it into the king's treasuries. And the king took his ring from his hand, and gave it unto Haman the son of Hammedatha the Agagite, the Jews' enemy. And the king said unto Haman, the silver is given to thee, the people also, to do with them as it seemeth good to thee. Then were the king's scribes called on the thirteenth day of the first month, and there was written according to all that Haman had commanded unto the king's lieutenants, and to the governors that were over every province, and to the rulers of every people of every province according to the writing thereof, and to every people after their language; in the name of king Ahasuerus was it written, and sealed with the king's ring. And the letters were sent by posts into all the king's provinces, to destroy, to kill, and to cause to perish, all Jews, both young and old, little children and women, in one day, even upon the thirteenth day of the twelfth month, which is the month Adar, and to take the spoil of them for a prey. The copy of the writing for a commandment to be given in every province was published unto all people, that they should be ready against that day. The posts went out, being hastened by the king's commandment, and the decree was given in Shushan the palace. And the king and Haman sat down to drink; but the city Shushan was perplexed" (Esther 3:5-15).

This is the yoke that made the multitude to rise against Christ and accused Him, and said that He had a devil – that Jesus Christ was gluttonous and a winebibber; a friend of the publicans and sinners.

"But whereunto shall I liken this generation? It is like unto children sitting in the markets, and calling unto their fellows, and saying, we have piped unto you, and ye have not danced; we have mourned unto you, and ye have not lamented. For John came neither eating nor drinking, and they say, He hath a devil. The Son of man came eating and drinking, and they say, Behold a man gluttonous, and a winebibber, a friend of publicans and sinners. But wisdom is justified of her children" (Matthew 11:16-19).

Because this yoke is the weapon of the devil upon the Pharisees, they also accused Jesus of casting out devils by Beelzebub's power; the prince of the devil.

> "Then was brought unto him one possessed with a devil, blind, and dumb: and he healed him, insomuch that the blind and dumb both spake and saw. And all the people were amazed, and said, Is not this the son of David? But when the Pharisees heard it, they said, this fellow doth not cast out devils, but by Beelzebub the prince of the devils" (Matthew 12:22-24).

This yoke also opposed Jesus, using the Pharisees and the Sadducees who really tempted Jesus seeking a sign. They later took counsel how they might entangle Him in speech. Even the Sadducees themselves said that there was nothing like resurrection. Moreover, the Pharisees accused Jesus of not observing the traditions of men. One of the Pharisees also told Him to depart from a particular place because Herod would kill Him.

"The same day there came certain of the Pharisees, saying unto him, get thee out, and depart hence: for Herod will kill thee. And he said unto them, go ye, and tell that fox, Behold, I cast out devils, and I do cures today and tomorrow, and the third day I shall be perfected" (Luke 13:31-32).

All the unbelieving chief priests, scribes and the elders assembled in the palace of Caiaphas, the high priest, and consulted how to arrest Christ subtly and kill Him.

"Then one of the twelve, called Judas Iscariot, went unto the chief priests... Then saith Jesus unto them, all ye shall be offended because of me this night: for it is written, I will smite the shepherd, and the sheep of the flock shall be scattered abroad... And, behold, one of them which were with Jesus stretched out his hand, and drew his sword, and struck a servant of the high priest's, and smote off his ear" (Matthew 26:14, 31, 51).

They persuaded the multitudes so that they should ask for the life of Barabbas to be spared while Christ should be destroyed.

"But the chief priests and elders persuaded the multitude that they should ask Barabbas, and destroy Jesus... So, they went, and made the sepulchre sure, sealing the stone, and setting a watch" (Matthew 27:20, 66).

The yoke of unbelief upon the life of Simon, the sorcerer, made him to bewitch a whole city of Samaria.

"But there was a certain man, called Simon, which before time in the same city used sorcery, and bewitched the people of Samaria, giving out that himself was some great one... Saying, Give me also this power, that on whomsoever I lay hands, he may receive the Holy Ghost" (Acts 8:9, 19).

The same yoke of unbelief energized Elymas to seek of a way to prevent his deputy from the knowledge of Christ.

"And when they had gone through the isle unto Paphos, they found a certain sorcerer, a false prophet, a Jew, whose name was Bar-jesus: Which was with the deputy of the country, Sergius Paulus, a prudent man; who called for Barnabas and Saul, and desired to hear the word of God. But Elymas the sorcerer (for so is his name by interpretation) withstood them, seeking to turn away the deputy from the faith" (Acts 13:6-8).

The yoke of unbelief upon the Gentiles made them to believe that once born again, there is no more back-sliding even if you go into sin – eternal security of a sinning saint.

"What shall we say then? Shall we continue in sin, that grace may abound? For in that he died, he died unto sin once: but in that he liveth, he liveth unto God" (Romans 6:1, 10).

This yoke upon the Greeks made them to seek wisdom outside Christ (See 1 Corinthians 1:22).

The yoke of unbelief makes people to fight against Christ. They are antichrist (See 1 Corinthians 16:22).

This yoke was used against some people in Thessalonica, and they refused to obey the gospel of Christ (See 2 Thessalonians 1:5:12).

When Paul went to Asia to preach, the people with the yoke of unbelief made others reject the gospel of Christ, and they turned away from him (See 2 Timothy 1:15).

The same yoke made Alexander, the coppersmith to withstand Paul's word during his ministry (See 2 Timothy 4:14-16).

This yoke does not allow people to believe God's word; doctrine, and his son Jesus Christ. In the days of Peter, this yoke made people to deny the Lord and became false prophets (See 2 Peter 2:1-3).

The major difference between the yoke of transgression and the yoke of unbelief is that the yoke of transgression is a yoke of sin, while the yoke of unbelief may allow her victim to be a sinner and yet still doubt everything about God.

The central theme of the Bible is Christ and Redemption (See Luke 24:25, 44-45). All the members of occults and false religions are unbelievers because they have one, two or more false beliefs about Christ. You cannot be a believer and have anything against Christ.

Jehovah Witnesses believe that Christ was a man, not more or less. God created Him and He is dead forever and suffered everlasting destruction, not resurrecting bodily. They are also classified as unbelievers. Christian Science says that Jesus was the divine idea of God i.e. Jesus Christ is not God. They don't believe the Bible, so they are also unbelievers. The Roman Catholics believe in purgatory, but the Bible says we have only Heaven and Hell. They have therefore deviated. They believe that prayers can be offered through Mary's name, and the dead saints. But the Scripture says that we can only pray through the name of Jesus (See John 14:13-14). Jesus Himself says He is the only way (See John 14:6). With this belief; they are also classified as unbelievers.

Rosicrucianism says that Christ is the highest initiate of the sun and not the only begotten Son of God. They are also wrong in their belief. They are also unbelievers. An unbeliever is not necessarily someone who sins greatly.

An unbeliever is not only people who do not go to church, neither is it only the idol worshippers. An unbeliever is someone whose belief is contrary to anything written in the Bible, especially against Christ. It is anybody whose doctrine or belief contradicts any section of the Bible. He may look very nice and can even be a philanthropist but once his belief contradicts the scripture, he or she is an unbeliever; and all unbelievers are candidates of hell fire. You may overcome every sin in life, but if any of your belief or doctrine is found to be contrary to the scripture, you will go to hell fire, because you have a yoke of unbelief.

"For I testify unto every man that heareth the words of the prophecy of this book, If any man shall add unto these things, God shall add unto him the plagues that are written in this book: And if any man shall take away from the words of the book of this prophecy, God shall

take away his part out of the book of life, and out of the
holy city, and from the things which are written in this
book" (Revelation 22:18-19).

You can overcome every manner of sin. You may live above reproach. You can even be a great minister; a general overseer or church founder with signs and wonders following you. Sin of all kinds may not be seen in your life both from God and man but if you have a false doctrinal belief or anything that contradicts any part of the Bible from Genesis to Revelation, you will go to hell fire, if you fail to repent and renounce such a doctrine. The yoke of unbelief is one of the most dangerous yokes in that it has taken so many great people to hell fire.

Even presently, many are being dragged to hell by this yoke. Please read the following passage carefully and meditate on it. Do not rush it; read it prayerfully and sincerely.

"Whosoever transgresseth, and abideth not in the
doctrine of Christ, hath not God. He that abideth in the

doctrine of Christ, he hath both the Father and the Son"
(2 John 1:9).

Mohammed, traditional religion, many saints, etc.; are not the Way; only Christ is the Way (John 14:6, 10:1, 18). For you to go to heaven, the yoke of unbelief must be broken in your life. In order not to die in unbelief, you have to believe the totality of God's word – the 39 books of the Old Testament and 27 books of the New Testament – as the inspired Word of God. You have to take the bible as the final authority in all matters concerning Christian conduct and work.

"All scripture is given by inspiration of God, and is profitable for doctrine, for reproof, for correction, for instruction in righteousness: That the man of God may be perfect, thoroughly furnished unto all good works" *(2 Timothy 3:16-17).*

CHAPTER 7

THE YOKE OF WOOD

The Webster Dictionary defines 'wood' as a dense growth of trees usually greater in extent than a grove; and smaller than a forest. It is often used in plants or construction. It is the hard-fibrous substance consisting basically of xylem that makes up the greater part of the stems; branches; and roots of trees or shrubs beneath the bark; found to a limited extent in herbaceous plants. Wood is suitable or prepared for use as burning or building.

"Go and tell Hananiah, saying, thus saith the LORD; Thou hast broken the yokes of wood; but thou shalt make for them yokes of iron" (Jeremiah 28:13).

The yoke of the wood is the weakest yoke among all the yokes. But even though it is weak, enemies have used it to destroy and render many lives useless. The yoke of the wood is the yoke of witchcraft. Witchcraft is one of the lowest in the rank of Satan; yet it has been used by Satan to destroy individuals; families and nations. The yoke of the wood has destroyed men and women of great destinies. The yoke of the wood is not strong in itself; but it uses ignorance and pretends to be something else that it is not. It can also destroy people's lives with intimidation, confusion, and manipulation. It can also be used in the form of force, or appear as if it is strong.

The yoke of the wood is the yoke of fear that magnifies itself bigger than the real size. With knowledge and faith in God; anybody; no matter how small; can easily; in a twinkle of an eye break the yoke of the wood.

"Then Hananiah the prophet took the yoke from off the prophet Jeremiah's neck, and break it" (Jeremiah 28:10).

Even the knowledgeable false prophets; native doctors and herbalists, can easily break the yoke of the wood.

Here are some of the examples of the yoke of the woods:

"Because of the multitude of the whoredoms of the well-favored harlot, the mistress of witchcrafts, that selleth nations through her whoredoms, and families through her witchcrafts" (Nahum 3:4).

These two powers are very small and weak but they are destructive: WITCHCRAFT AND WHOREDOMS (meaning prostitution). These are the two powers that destroyed Solomon and made a caricature of his wisdom and greatness.

"But king Solomon loved many strange women, together with the daughter of Pharaoh, women of the Moabites, Ammonites, Edomites, Zidonians, and Hittites; of the nations concerning which the LORD said unto the children of Israel, Ye shall not go in to them, neither shall they come in unto you: for surely they will turn away your heart after their gods: Solomon clave unto these in love. And he had seven hundred wives, princesses, and three hundred concubines: and his wives turned away his heart. For it came to pass, when Solomon was old, that his wives turned away his heart after other gods: and his heart was not perfect with the LORD his God, as was the heart of David his father. For Solomon went after Ashtoreth the goddess of the Zidonians, and after Milcom the abomination of the Ammonites. And Solomon did evil in the sight of the LORD, and went not fully after the LORD, as did David his father. Then

did Solomon build a high place for Chemosh, the abomination of Moab, in the hill that is before Jerusalem, and for Molech, the abomination of the children of Ammon. And likewise, did he for all his strange wives, which burnt incense and sacrificed unto their gods" (1 Kings 11:1-8).

The acts of immorality look very innocent and harmless at the start. It tastes like sugar and honey but the end is bitter. It is the yoke of the wood. The appearance of the yoke of the wood is not harmful at all. They are inviting and lovely. They can flatter with their tongue. They look very beautiful with innocent eyelids of lust. They can reduce a great person to a piece of bread.

"To keep thee from the evil woman, from the flattery of the tongue of a strange woman. For by means of a whorish woman a man is brought to a piece of bread: and the adulteress will hunt for the precious life. But whoso committeth adultery with a woman lacketh

understanding: he that doeth it destroyeth his own soul" (Proverbs 6:24, 26, 32).

The yoke of wood is contagious. It can destroy massively through yoking just one person. It is the yoke of HIV/AIDS, EBOLA OR CORONAVIRUS and other infectious diseases. A prostitute either commercial or private can stay in a hotel or hostel and yet with this yoke connect people's lives and destinies all over the continents of the world through sexual evil transfer.

"Because of the multitude of the whoredoms of the well-favored harlot, the mistress of witchcrafts, that selleth nations through her whoredoms, and families through her witchcrafts" (Nahum 3:4).

This is the power that destroyed the children of Israel in their numbers in the wilderness.

"And Israel abode in Shittim, and the people began to commit whoredom with the daughters of Moab… And Israel joined himself unto Baal–peor: and the anger of the LORD was kindled against Israel" (Numbers 25:1, 3).

Sodom and Gomorrah received the judgment of the rain of fire from heaven because of the yoke of the wood.

"And there came two angels to Sodom at even; and Lot sat in the gate of Sodom: and Lot seeing them rose up to meet them; and he bowed himself with his face toward the ground… And he pressed upon them greatly; and they turned in unto him, and entered into his house; and he made them a feast, and did bake unleavened bread, and they did eat. But before they lay down, the men of the city, even the men of Sodom, compassed the house round, both old and young, all the people from

every quarter: And they called unto Lot, and said unto him, where are the men which came in to thee this night? Bring them out unto us, that we may know them" (Genesis 19:1, 3-5).

This is the power that killed all the males in Shechem (See Genesis 34:25). This power also wasted the lives of all men and women who had ever had sexual relationship in sin (See Numbers 3:13-14). This power also destroyed the strongest man upon the earth after taking away his two eyes (See Judges 16:11, 27, 31). This power also destroyed 65,000 men in Israel just because of a prostitute (See Judges 19:22-30; 20:11-45).

Jezebel who was also a great witch later died under this yoke. After bewitching others, she was bewitched also (See 2 Kings 9:30-37). The yoke is presently in the church killing many people silently and unnoticed (See 1 Corinthians 5:1-12).

The yoke of the wood is the yoke of witchcraft all over the world. It is the power of immorality – little sin left alone or neglected in any life (See Songs of Solomon 2:15).

CHAPTER 8

BELIEVER'S YOKES BROKEN BY GOD

Many a time, believers may seem to forget God in the midst of their problems. Satan's presence in the lives of some people makes them forget the past divine interventions. They focus on their problem instead of God; and when such things happen, their faith in God will be affected.

Our God is a yoke breaker. No matter how wicked, strong or how long you have encountered your problem God is able to break it. If you have faith in God, no matter your situation, God can break your yoke and promote you beyond your expectations. In the days of Abel, by faith, Abel offered burnt offerings to God and God had respect for his sacrifices. The yoke of evil sacrifices that caged his generation could not cage him.

In the days of Enoch, he believed God, and God broke the yoke of iniquity in his life. He was the only person in his time that walked with God for about three hundred years.

The yoke of mass destruction that caged Noah's generation could not affect him. He was the only righteous and by God's grace he overcame the yoke of mass destruction. Abraham broke the yoke of idolatry to answer God's call in his generation. The Lord also broke the yoke of barrenness in his life and family, and Sarah, his wife gave birth to Isaac.

The Lord broke the yoke of imprisonment in the life of Joseph and made him the Prime Minister in a foreign land. God broke the yoke of the Egyptian bondage and the children of Israel were set free. God has done so many great things that are enough to convince his children that with Him, every yoke can be broken. It is an insult for a believer to question the ability of God to break any yoke.

When the yoke of death was placed upon Moses, many people were looking for his life for destruction. When God broke the yoke of death in the life of Moses all the men that sought to kill him, who also refused to repent, died.

"And the LORD said unto Moses in Midian, Go, return into Egypt: for all the men are dead which sought thy life" (Exodus 4:19).

The same yoke that God broke in the life of Moses was used to yoke the entire first born of Egypt unto death. Satan used this same yoke that was broken in the lives of Moses and the children of Israel, and the host of the Egyptian army was overthrown in the Red Sea, including Pharaoh.

"And the children of Israel went into the midst of the sea upon the dry ground: and the waters were a wall unto them on their right hand, and on their left. And the Egyptians pursued, and went in after them to the midst of the sea, even all Pharaoh's horses, his chariots, and his horsemen. And it came to pass, that in the morning watch the LORD looked unto the host of the Egyptians through the pillar of fire and of the cloud, and troubled the host of the Egyptians, And took off their chariot wheels, that they drave them heavily: so that the Egyptians said, Let us flee from the face of Israel; for the LORD fighteth for them against the Egyptians. And the LORD said unto Moses, stretch out thine hand over the sea, that the waters may come again upon the Egyptians, upon their chariots, and upon their horsemen. And Moses stretched forth his hand over the sea, and the sea returned to his strength when the morning appeared; and the Egyptians fled against it; and the LORD overthrew the Egyptians in the midst of the sea. And the waters returned, and covered the chariots, and the horsemen, and all the host of Pharaoh

that came into the sea after them; there remained not so much as one of them. But the children of Israel walked upon dry land in the midst of the sea; and the waters were a wall unto them on their right hand, and on their left. Thus, the LORD saved Israel that day out of the hand of the Egyptians; and Israel saw the Egyptians dead upon the seashore. And Israel saw that great work which the LORD did upon the Egyptians: and the people feared the LORD, and believed the LORD, and his servant Moses" (Exodus 14:22-31).

The children of Israel who received the divine favor of breaking yoke from God later despised God to gather manna on the Sabbath day.

"And it came to pass, that there went out some of the people on the seventh day for to gather, and they found none" (Exodus 16:27).

They forced Aaron to make an idol, which they also worshipped. They later complained over a little problem and it displeases God.

> *"And when the people complained, it displeased the LORD: and the LORD heard it; and his anger was kindled; and the fire of the LORD burnt among them, and consumed them that were in the uttermost parts of the camp"* (Numbers 11:1).

The ten spies forgot all the yokes of Egypt that God broke over their lives. They also forgot God and discouraged the hearts of the people (See Number 13:26, 29, 31, 33). They all became afraid over a minor issue and forgot God who dealt with the satanic yokes in their lives.

Korah, Dathan, and Abiriam rebelled against Moses, and caused division in the camp of the children of God. They failed to trust the Lord who had solved bigger problems in their lives. Our God and our Yoke-breaker came back to them in their backslidden state. He introduced himself as the Lord God, which brought them forth out of the land of Egypt. The yoke of the bondage in Egypt under Pharaoh was a yoke of slavery unto death yet God delivered them.

"I am the LORD your God, which brought you forth out of the land of Egypt, that ye should not be their bondmen; and I have broken the bands of your yoke, and made you go upright" (Leviticus 26:13).

When God delivers a believer and breaks his yoke, he should not submit to any other yoke. However, if he finds himself under any other yoke; the God who delivered him at first is ready to forgive and deliver him if he only returns to God and forsakes his sin with determination to please God at all cost. He should have faith in God and believe that with God all things are possible. Believers should not fear any yoke; no matter how that yoke is. Once you believe God, no evil yoke can prevail over you.

Believers should therefore reject every form of bondage in life. We should not submit to any problem in life. Yokes are not meant to keep a true believer in bondage for a long time. Every believer should go to God and believing that God can break their yokes. We should not as believers submit to any evil power or ugly situation. God wants every believer to reign over every evil power; no matter what they have achieved in the lives of others. We are delivered to stand upright before every opposing enemy, problem, or power.

True believers are not meant to remain under any form of oppression of any oppressor. God promised to take away every burden from the believer's life (See Matthew 11:28). The rod of the oppressor is not meant to remain permanent in any true believer's life. Our God is ready to do away with any problem confronting every true Christian. He did it before; He is still doing it today; and He promised to do it for all who will trust Him. Our God still breaks the yoke of every believer. Those who trust in God do not live long under any yoke.

"And Zacchæus stood, and said unto the Lord; Behold, Lord, the half of my goods I give to the poor; and if I have taken anything from any man by false accusation, I restore him fourfold… For the Son of man is come to seek and to save that which was lost" (Luke 19:8, 10).

The original plan and desires of God is that no true believer should die under any kind of yoke. He wants every believer to be presented to Him without blemish; both spiritually and physically (See Numbers 19:2).

The anointing of God on believers is meant to break every evil yoke. The reason why God anoints believers is for them to use it in breaking yokes. The anointing upon you as a believer can break every manner of yoke once your faith agrees with the word of God. Anointing of God is a true enemy of all kinds of yoke.

"And it shall come to pass in that day, that his burden shall be taken away from off thy shoulder, and his yoke

from off thy neck, and the yoke shall be destroyed because of the anointing" (Isaiah 10:27).

Among the children of God, He desires that the yokes of the Assyrians and their burdens should not be seen in the lives of true believers.

"That I will break the Assyrian in my land, and upon my mountains tread him under foot: then shall his yoke depart from off them, and his burden depart from off their shoulders" (Isaiah 14:25).

No believer is destined to remain under any evil oppression. If we fast at all times as believers, it should be directed at loosing the bands of wickedness around us; to undo the heavy burdens; to let the oppressed go free; and to break every yoke.

"Is not this the fast that I have chosen? To loose the bands of wickedness, to undo the heavy burdens, and to let the oppressed go free, and that ye break every yoke?" (Isaiah 58:6).

The Lord has given every believer the power to take away every yoke. It makes God's heart happy if yokes of problems are taken away from among His people. He delights in believers who help to take yokes away in the midst of true believers.

"Then shalt thou call, and the LORD shall answer; thou shalt cry, and he shall say, Here I am. If thou take away from the midst of thee the yoke, the putting forth of the finger, and speaking vanity" (Isaiah 58:9).

From the ancient days, God has always been in the business of breaking evil yokes. He does not condone evil bands. Our God is a yoke-breaker right from the beginning.

"For of old time I have broken thy yoke, and burst thy bands; and thou saidst, I will not transgress; when upon every high hill and under every green tree thou wanderest, playing the harlot" (Jeremiah 2:20).

God regards people who are engaged in breaking yoke as great people; the people who know the way of God.

"For it shall come to pass in that day, saith the LORD of hosts, that I will break his yoke from off thy neck, and will burst thy bonds, and strangers shall no more serve themselves of him" (Jeremiah 30:8).

If you as a believer cannot directly break your yoke, then believe that God can do it. What He needs is your faith. Every creature rejoices when God breaks evil yokes. Things go on well when God breaks yokes. With evil yokes broken, the earth always experiences increase and safety in the land. Knowledge of God always increases whenever God breaks yokes. Whenever God breaks evil yokes, the eaters of flesh, the drinkers of blood and destiny destroyers are always exposed (See Ezekiel 34:27).

HOW TO BREAK YOUR EVIL YOKES BY FAITH AND BY PRAYERS

In most cases when a true believer or a person who is born again newly is in trouble, God always looks for his or her faith. Once such a person has faith in Christ, his yokes will be broken. Most of the time, it is faith that breaks the yoke.

"And he said unto her, Daughter, thy faith hath made thee whole; go in peace, and be whole of thy plague" *(Mark 5:34).*

Faith in Christ comes out from the victims of yokes before yokes are broken (See Mark 10:52).

When the little baby who was cast out as an illegitimate child cried, God heard his voice right in the wilderness; and the yoke of isolation, rejection, poverty and death in his life was broken.

And Abraham rose up early in the morning, and took bread, and a bottle of water, and gave it unto Hagar, putting it on her shoulder, and the child, and sent her away: and she departed, and wandered in the wilderness of Beersheba. And the water was spent in the bottle, and she cast the child under one of the shrubs. And she went, and sat her down over against him a good way off, as it were a bowshot: for she said, let me not see the death of the child. And she sat over against him, and lift up her voice, and wept. And God heard the voice of the lad; and the angel of God called to Hagar out of heaven, and said unto her, what aileth thee, Hagar? fear not; for God hath heard the voice of the lad where he is. Arise, lift up the lad, and hold him in thine hand; for I will make him a great nation. And God opened her eyes, and she saw a well of water; and she went, and filled the bottle with water, and gave the lad drink Genesis 21:14-19).

Through prayers the evil yokes attached to the name of Jacob was broken and his name was changed from Jacob to Israel (See Genesis 35:14-15).

The prayers of the children of Israel attracted divine attention. God remembered his covenant with Abraham, Isaac, and Jacob. They cried and God came down and broke their Egyptian bondage (See Exodus 2:23, 25).

Jabez prayed in faith, and God broke the age-long poverty in his father's house 1 Chronicles 4:9-10 ...

When everybody, including Isaiah confirmed that God was determined to take away the life of Hezekiah, it was faith and prayers that saved the situation. After the prayer of faith in righteousness; God healed him and added fifteen years to his life; minus sorrow, headache, and any form of infirmities for those fifteen years.

In those days was Hezekiah sick unto death. And Isaiah the prophet the son of Amoz came unto him, and said unto him, thus saith the Lord, set thine

house in order: for thou shalt die, and not live.
Then Hezekiah turned his face toward the wall, and
prayed unto the Lord, ... Go, and say to Hezekiah,
thus saith the Lord, the God of David thy father, I
have heard thy prayer, I have seen thy tears:
behold, I will add unto thy days fifteen years (Isaiah
38:1-2, 5).

Elijah prayed in faith and God answered him by fire.
God's answer broke the yoke of false worship in Israel;
and gave rain to the whole nation after three years and
six months (See 2 Kings 18:1-46). Jehoshaphat and all
Judah prayed and fasted in faith; and God broke the yoke
of the enemies in their nation (See 2 Chronicles 20:1-2).
Mordecai, Esther and all the children of Israel in captivity
prayed and cried to God in faith and God broke the yoke
of death decree pronounced against them (See Esther
4:16).

The yoke of the devil can be broken by prayers and
fasting. Once one repents of every sin and forsakes them,

with prayers coupled with faith in Christ, every yoke of his life can be broken (See Matthew 17:21; Mark 9:23).

God is a prayer answering God; and once a true Christian goes into prayers; believing God for breaking yokes; all his yokes will be broken.

"And one of the malefactors which were hanged railed on him, saying, if thou be Christ, save thyself and us. But the other answering rebuked him, saying, Dost not thou fear God, seeing thou art in the same condemnation? And we indeed justly; for we receive the due reward of our deeds: but this man hath done nothing amiss. And he said unto Jesus, Lord, remember me when thou comest into thy kingdom. And Jesus said unto him, Verily I say unto thee, today shalt thou be with me in paradise" (Luke 23:39-43).

When the international criminal on the cross realized his sins; repented and confessed them with prayers of request; Jesus broke the yoke of transgressions, sorrows, death, and hell fire immediately in his life and took him to paradise. What a wonderful opportunity! Yokes are broken when sincere prayers are offered to God in faith. I challenge you to begin to pray and your yokes shall be broken by fire.

BY UNDERSTANDING HOW TO PRAISE GOD

The scripture says that we should not be mindful to anything; but by prayers and supplication, with thanksgiving let our request be made known unto God. As true believers, no matter what happens to us; we should not fret or have any anxiety. We as believers, in any circumstances, should pray and define our problems to God with thanksgiving.

"Be careful for nothing; but in everything by prayer and supplication with thanksgiving let your requests be made known unto God" (Philippians 4:6).

At midnight hours; almost at the time of satanic execution; the exact time that Paul and Silas were meant to be killed; they started songs of praise to God. If they had failed to praise God in the prison, they would have been executed. In any situation we should sing praises unto God. God has used the hymns of praise to break many yokes. These two young men sang until other prisoners heard it.

As they were still singing, the Lord sent a great earthquake to break their yokes. Their praises attracted divine earthquake that touched the very foundations of the prison house. Every place was shaking, suddenly, and without delay, their yokes were broken. The power of God was released; and immediately, all the doors of the prison were opened; while at the same time, everyone's chains were unfastened and loosed. As the prison doors got opened everyone's bands were loosed instantly.

All their yokes were broken just by singing praises. The power of God awoke all the keepers. They were startled out of their sleep. They woke up to see the broken yokes on the true believers. This hour is your own midnight. You can break your own yokes.

"And at midnight Paul and Silas prayed, and sang praises unto God: and the prisoners heard them and suddenly there was a great earthquake, so that the foundations of the prison were shaken: and immediately all the doors were opened, and everyone's bands were loosed. And the keeper of the prison awaking out of his sleep, and seeing the prison doors open, he drew out his sword, and would have killed himself; supposing that the prisoners had been freed" (Acts 16:25-27).

When a true believer understands how to sing and praise God his yokes can easily be broken. Every battle is not meant to be fought with just any weapon. We must approach our God for directives. We may not use physical weapon at times. Our weapons are not carnal

(See 2 Corinthians 10:4). Some yokes are meant to be broken directly by God.

> *"Then upon Jahaziel the son of Zechariah, the son of Benaiah, the son of Jeiel, the son of Mattaniah, a Levite of the sons of Asaph, came the Spirit of the LORD in the midst of the congregation; And he said, Hearken ye, all Judah, and ye inhabitants of Jerusalem, and thou king Jehoshaphat, Thus saith the LORD unto you, Be not afraid nor dismayed by reason of this great multitude; for the battle t:~ not yours, but God's. Tomorrow go ye down against them: behold, they come up by the cliff of Ziz; and ye shall find them at the end of the brook, before the wilderness of Jeruel"* (2 Chronicles 20:14-16).

We may need to pray a little and sing praises in the battlefield; and our yokes can then be broken. When we know how to sing, we need not to fear any yoke or be dismayed. When we sing pure and undefiled praises unto

God with faith, God will break our yoke and show us his true salvation (See 2 Chronicles 20:17-19).

True worship attracts divine attention. King Jehoshaphat bowed his head with his face to the ground and all the inhabitants of Jerusalem big and small fell before the Lord, all worshipping the only true God. Our God is touched when believers approached Him with praises and worship (2 Chronicles 20:20-23).

"And they rose early in the morning, and went forth into the wilderness of Tekoa: and as they went forth, Jehoshaphat stood and said, Hear me, O Judah, and ye inhabitants of Jerusalem; Believe in the LORD your God, so shall ye be established; believe his prophets, so shall ye prosper. And when he had consulted with the people, he appointed singers unto the LORD, and that should praise the beauty of holiness, as they went out before the army, and to say, Praise the LORD; for his mercy endureth forever. And when they began to sing and to praise, the LORD set ambushments against the

children of Ammon, Moab, and mount Seir, which were come against Judah; and they were smitten. For the children of Ammon and Moab stood up against the inhabitants of mount Seir, utterly to slay and destroy them: and when they had made an end of the inhabitants of Seir, every one helped to destroy another" (2 Chronicles 20:20-23).

Praises and worship break every evil yoke and lays ambush against our enemies. It causes division among united evil groups. It can break every evil yoke and set captives and believers free. Praise and worships are great weapons of breaking yokes in the life of a true believer.

REMOVAL OF EVERY IDOL

Idolatry is a great sin against God. God was angry with Aaron when he led the people of God into idolatry. Balaam who was instrumental in the children of God falling into immorality and idolatry was punished by God (See Numbers 23, 24).

Egyptians and other nations of the world who worshipped idols were severally punished. God's anger fell upon them (See Deuteronomy 29:12-29). Do away with every idol; both spiritual and physical. We must destroy every personal idol possession (See Acts 19:18-20).

Believers who wish that their yoke be broken should do away with occult materials. We must make full confession and thoroughly expose all our former deception and evil practices. All those who had practiced sorcery and magic should expose their materials for destruction. Before a believer's yokes will be fully broken, he must do away with any property belonging to idol worship.

Finally, we must live a holy life; not fighting our Jacob with canal weapons; but watching and praying for our dominion to come. There is a time appointed by God for our dominion. If we watch, pray and discover such time of our dominion, our yokes shall be broken.

> *"And by thy sword shalt thou live, and shalt serve thy brother; and it shall come to pass when thou shalt have the dominion, that thou shalt break leis yoke from off thy neck" (Genesis 27:40).*

If we are spiritual and sensitive to the voice of the Holy Ghost, we shall know exactly when our yokes shall be broken. God has appointed this time for every believer to grow restive so as to break, loose and tear his yoke from his life. We need to be in the spirit always, in order to discover such time with prayers of faith, praise and worship, and total removal of all idols. So shall our yokes be broken (See Isaiah 10:27).

ENCOUNTER WITH THE ONLY TRUE YOKE

Every man without exception is born with a heavy load of problem (Job 14:1; Psalms 51: 5). Jesus Christ, who is God Himself is the only Person that has the power to deliver mankind from the problems of life.

> *"Come unto me, all ye that labor and are heavy laden, and I will give you rest" (Matthew 11:28).*

Without response to this universal call, no one can make it in life. To overcome every evil yoke and live successfully in this life, we must take the yoke of Christ. The yoke of Christ is the easiest yoke in life. His own yoke offers rest while others increase people's burdens in life. The yoke of Christ sends rest right into peoples' souls and makes his burden light.

"Take my yoke upon you, and learn of me; for I am meek and lowly in heart: and ye shall find rest unto your souls" (Matthew 11:29).

The yoke of the Lord binds man with God into eternity. Once you are yoked with Christ you are bound to succeed in life and in death.

It is true that Abel died young, but the yoke of God upon his life took him up to divine presence and his blood cried for revenge. You cannot defeat anybody who is yoked to the Lord, either in life or death. When Enoch came into contact with this yoke, he walked with God without any interruption for 300 years. Through this yoke, he became the first man on earth to be raptured. God took him up to heaven without death. This yoke singled Noah out from his generation and he survived the flood. This yoke drew Abraham out of evil foundation and made him the father of many nations. This yoke kept Joseph in this evil world and he lived for 110 years with many evidences that he pleased God. When this yoke once came upon Lot, he was able to entertain the angels of God.

With the Lord's yoke, Jacob prayed down the anger of Esau his twin brother. With this yoke upon Joseph, he rejected a free offer of immorality and later became a Prime Minister and leader to all his enemies. With this yoke upon the parents of Moses in Egypt, they refused to kill their son, Moses. With this yoke, the serpent of Moses swallowed all the serpents of the magicians of Egypt.

With this yoke upon the children of Israel they all crossed the Red Sea and saw the death of their enemies. When this yoke is upon you, you will win every battle of life.

With this yoke upon Caleb and Joshua they believed God and manifested faith in Israel. With this yoke, the daughters of Zelophehad sued for their father's inheritance and recovered them (Numbers 27: 1-11). With this yoke upon the whole nation of Israel God fulfilled all his promises to them.

And the Lord gave unto Israel all the land which he sware to give unto their fathers; and they possessed it, and dwelt therein. And the Lord gave them rest round about, according to all that he sware unto their fathers: and there stood not a man of all their enemies before them; the Lord delivered all their enemies into their hand. There failed not ought of any good thing which the Lord had spoken unto the house of Israel; all came to pass (Joshua 21:43-45).

With this yoke upon Elisha, he asked and received the double portion anointing of his master, Elijah. With this yoke upon Joseph, he obeyed the voice of an angel and retained the mother of his own savior.

"And when they were departed, behold, the angel of the Lord appeareth to Joseph in a dream, saying, Arise, and take the young child and his mother, and flee into Egypt, and be thou there until I bring thee word: for Herod will seek the young child to destroy him. When

he arose, he took the young child and his mother by night, and departed into Egypt: And was there until the death of Herod: that it might be fulfilled which was spoken of the Lord by the prophet, saying, Out of Egypt have I called my son" (Matthew 2:13-15).

With this yoke, Peter walked on the sea with Jesus.

"And Peter answered him and said, Lord, if it be thou, bid me come unto thee on the water. And he said, come. And when Peter was come down out of the ship, he walked on the water, to go to Jesus" (Matthew 14:28-29).

With this yoke upon you, you can break every evil yoke. You can walk upon the sea in the midst of witchcraft powers. You can overcome every problem of life and live your life pleasing only God. With this yoke, all things are possible. The yoke of Christ is a yoke above every other yoke.

Through this yoke, you can break the yoke of the neck, the yoke of iron, and oxen. With this yoke, you can break the heavy yoke upon your life. With this yoke, you can do away with every grievous yoke.

The yoke of Christ cannot tolerate the yoke of the king of Babylon, Egypt, the yoke of transgression and the yoke of the wood. When you confront the yoke of the Jaws, the yoke of the youth or unbelief, they will bow to divine yoke. This is the only yoke approved by God. This is the only yoke that can give you rest in your soul and make difficult things easy for you in life. Take this yoke today and your life will be transformed. Jesus has sent a universal invitation to everyone who will come and take this yoke.

"Come unto me, all ye that labor and are heavy laden, and I will give you rest Take my yoke upon you, and learn of me. For I am meek and lowly in heart: and ye

shall find rest unto your souls. For my yoke is easy, and my burden is light" (Matthew 11:28-30).

PRAYER WARFARE SECTION

Below are 271 prayer points of enough is enough. Handle it daily until you finish prayer all of them one after the other. Don't rush each number, pray until you are satisfied with each number, even if it takes you months to finish praying all of them. Don't just recite it, pray each one aggressively until something happen. Confess your sins, give your life to Christ before praying. Am with you in the Spirit as you pray.

271 ENOUGH IS ENOUGH PRAYERS

1. Any spiritual wooden bar or flame yoking me together with any witchcraft animal, break, in the name of Jesus.

2. Let the powers of darkness keeping me in bondage be destroyed, in the name of Jesus.

3. Any evil device placed upon my life to control my me, break to pieces, in the name of Jesus.

4. Every yoke of captivity placed upon my life, break by fire, in the name of Jesus.

5. Owners of evil load upon my shoulder, carry your load now, in the name of Jesus.

6. All evil loads that are suspended upon any part of my body, I drop you by force, in the name of Jesus.

7. You my head, reject every evil load now, in the name of Jesus.

8. Father Lord, break every evil load upon my life

from the queen of heaven, in the name of Jesus.

9. Let the satanic instrument hanging evil load in my life be roasted by fire, in the name of Jesus.

10. I break and loose myself from every evil unity, in the name of Jesus.

11. I break and loose myself from collective captivity, in the name of Jesus.

12. Let the entire oppressive agency in my life be oppressed by fire, in the name of Jesus.

13. Every yoke of slavery upon my life, break by fire, in the name of Jesus

14. Every oppressive agency linking me up to any problem, receive destruction, in the name of Jesus.

15. You my personal yoke, begin to break now, in the name of Jesus.

16. Let all my family yoke attacking my life break to pieces, in the name of Jesus.

17. Father Lord, break to pieces my entire tribal yokes, in the name of Jesus.

18. You, the environmental yoke keeping me in bondage, break by fire, in the name of Jesus.

19. Every evil burden of my life, be roasted by fire, in the name of Jesus.

20. Let all my worrisome situations begin to disappear, in the name of Jesus.

21. Any power that constitutes problems in my life, die, in the name of Jesus.

22. Let that power that is restricting my progress be destroyed, in the name of Jesus.

23. Any wicked device that reduces my divine impute, be roasted by fire, in the name of Jesus.

24. Any evil power that is forcing me into defeat, die, in the name of Jesus.

25. Any control device of the enemy over my life, be destroyed, in the name of Jesus.

26. You, powers of perpetual bondage in my life, disappear from my life, in the name of Jesus.

27. Let the presence of oppressors in my family disappear, in the name of Jesus.

28. I remover evil limitations upon my life, in the name of Jesus.

29. Any Pharaoh that is oppressing my life, fall down and die, in the name of Jesus.

30. Father Lord, remove every power that wants to convert me into a slave, in the name of Jesus.

31. Lord Jesus, break every yoke asking me who is my God, in the name of Jesus.

32. Any powers in my life that is mocking my God, die, in the name of Jesus.

33. You, stubborn Pharaoh, fall down and die, in the name of Jesus.

34. Any evil yoke that is destroying my Promised Land, break by force, in the name of Jesus.

35. Every stubborn yoke in my life, break to pieces, in the name of Jesus.

36. Every occult yoke that was placed upon my life, break, in the name of Jesus.

37. I bind and cast out inherited evil spirits, in the name of Jesus.

38. Any power that wants to keep me in the land of Egypt, release me and die, in the name of Jesus.

39. Every yoke of idolatry in my life, break by fire, in the name of Jesus.

40. Every yoke of sickness in my life, break, in the name of Jesus.

41. Every yoke of sin in my life, break by fire, in the name of Jesus.

42. Every yoke of incurable disease in my life, break, in the name of Jesus.

43. Every yoke of Satan that is delaying my journey into the Promise Land, break, in the name of Jesus.

44.   Every yoke of defeats upon my life, break, in the name of Jesus.

45.   Let yokes of evil diversion upon my life begin to break, in the name of Jesus.

46.   Every yoke of desert life upon my life, break by fire, in the name of Jesus.

47.   Father Lord, break yokes of curses that was placed upon my destiny, in the name of Jesus.

48.   I destroy every yoke of iniquity upon my life, in the name of Jesus.

49.   Let all mysterious problems in my life disappear, in the name of Jesus.

50.   Let the yoke of affliction placed upon my life disappear, in the name of Jesus.

51.   Let the yoke of chronic problems upon my life begin to break, in the name of Jesus.

52.   Every yoke of uncontrollable desires for evil upon

my destiny, break by fire, in the name of Jesus.

53. Every yoke of marriage breakup in my family line, break now, in the name of Jesus.

54. You, yoke of late marriage upon my life, break now, in the name of Jesus.

55. All you yoke of business failures in my life, break, in the name of Jesus.

56. Every yoke of sudden disappearance of good helpers, break by fire, in the name of Jesus.

57. Every yoke of barrenness upon my life, break by fire, in the name of Jesus

58. Every yoke of miscarriage, break by fire, in the name of Jesus.

59. Every yoke that is prevention my conception, break by fire, in the name of Jesus.

60. Every yoke of suffering upon my life, break, in the name of Jesus.

61. Let the yoke of agony, pains and troubles upon

my life be broken, in the name of Jesus.

62.   Every visible and invisible yoke upon my life, be broken by fire, in the name of Jesus.

63.   Every yoke of financial problems in my life, break by fire, in the name of Jesus.

64.   Every yoke of sleeplessness upon my life, break, in the name of Jesus.

65.   Let the yoke of evil addiction upon my life be destroyed by fire, in the name of Jesus.

66.   Let all determined slave masters fall down and die, in the name of Jesus.

67.   I break to pieces iron gates that are keeping me behind inheritance, in the name of Jesus.

68.   I break to pieces every evil key that is locking up my destiny, in the name of Jesus.

69.   Father Lord, break the yoke of ill health upon my life, in the name of Jesus.

70.   Any power that is holding my breakthrough,

scatter, in the name of Jesus.

71. I break every witchcraft padlock in my destiny, in the name of Jesus

72. I open by force the prison gate over my ministry, in the name of Jesus.

73. I break every yoke of worldliness against my life, in the name of Jesus.

74. Let yokes of my old evil ways of life be broken by fire, in the name of Jesus.

75. O Lord, send heavenly assistance to break evil yokes in my life, in the name of Jesus.

76. Any evil yoke that is stealing good things out of my life, be broken by fire, in the name of Jesus.

77. Lord Jesus, pass me through the iron gates of my life, in the name of Jesus.

78. Let my business, marriage, etc., pass through the iron gates of hell by fire, in the name of Jesus.

79. Any power that is holding my character in

bondage, release it and die, in the name of Jesus.

80. You, satanic yokes that are holding my anointing, break, in the name of Jesus.

81. You, the Goliath of my destiny, die, die, die, in the name of Jesus.

82. You, my Israel in bondage, be released now, in the name of Jesus.

83. O Lord that broke the yoke of Jabez, break my yoke by fire, in the name of Jesus.

84. Father Lord, enlarge my coast and destroy my sorrows, in the name of Jesus.

85. You, my Peter in the bondage, come out by fire, in the name of Jesus.

86. Every yoke of death upon my life, break by fire, in the name of Jesus.

87. Every yoke of hell fire upon my life, break to pieces, in the name of Jesus.

88. Every yoke of Haman upon my family, break, in

the name of Jesus.

89. Every yoke of polygamy upon my life, break, in the name of Jesus.

90. I break the yoke of leprosy on my life, in the name of Jesus.

91. O Lord, break my yokes and make me great, in the name of Jesus.

92. O Lord, break my yokes and kill my giants, in the name of Jesus.

93. Any satanic yoke upon my neck, break to pieces, in the name of Jesus.

94. O Lord, break my yokes and take me to my divine destination, in the name of Jesus.

95. I break my yoke and turn myself towards the right destination, in the name of Jesus.

96. Any evil yoke that is misdirecting my life, break now, in the name of Jesus.

97. Any evil yoke that is causing me to serve

strangers, break to pieces, in the name of Jesus.

98.   Any evil yoke that is taking me to the camp of my enemies, break, in the name of Jesus.

99.   Let evil yoke of tradition, custom and false doctrine in my life break, in the name of Jesus.

100.   Every yoke of fear upon my life, break, in the name of Jesus.

101.   1 destroy yokes of falsehood upon my life, in the name of Jesus

102.   Any yoke that is determined to make my life useless, break, in the name of Jesus.

103.   Let all spiritual and physical yokes in my life be broken by fire, in the name of Jesus.

104.   Any yoke that is separating me from God's grace, break, in the name of Jesus.

105.   Every yoke of the enemy upon my life, break immediately, in the name of Jesus.

106.   You, the band of my yokes, break, in the name of

Jesus.

107. Every yoke of family bondage and destruction, break by fire, in the name of Jesus.

108. Every yoke of famine and destruction upon my life, break, in the name of Jesus.

109. Any evil yoke that is locking up my heavens, break, in the name of Jesus.

110. Let the hardened yokes in my life begin to break to pieces, in the name of Jesus.

111. Every yoke of unfriendly friends in my life, break to pieces, in the name of Jesus.

112. Every yoke of hunger and thirst in my life, break by fire, in the name of Jesus.

113. Let the yoke of nakedness upon my life break by fire, in the name of Jesus.

114. Every yoke of death upon my life, break, in the name of Jesus.

115. Every yoke of grave and hell upon my life, break

by fire, in the name of Jesus.

116.   I break the yoke of abject poverty upon my life, in the name of Jesus.

117.   I break and lose myself from local and international yokes, in the name of Jesus.

118.   I break any yoke that wants to enslave me to evil prosperity, in the name of Jesus.

119.   I break and loose myself from the yoke of common errors, in the name of Jesus.

120.   Father Lord, deliver me from yokes of evil influence, in the name of Jesus.

121.   Every yoke of false worship upon my life, break, in the name of Jesus.

122.   I break every yoke that is using the sun, moon, stars and other elements against my life, in the name of Jesus.

123.   I break and loose myself from every yoke of oxen and bull, in the name of Jesus.

124.   Any satanic yoke that is fashioned to deprive me of my blessings, break, in the name of Jesus.

125.   Let evil yokes that attack ovaries break for my sake, in the name of Jesus.

126.   Let that power that was assigned to castrate me die, in the name of Jesus.

127.   Any yoke that was assigned to render me impotent, break by force, in the name of Jesus.

128.   Any yoke that is attacking my vitality, die by fire, in the name of Jesus.

129.   I break and loose my destiny from evil yokes, in the name of Jesus.

130.   Father Lord, destroy yoke of oxen upon my life, in the name of Jesus.

131.   Any yoke that is assigned to siphon me physical and spiritually, break by fire, in the name of Jesus.

132.   Any occult grand master that is attacking my life with evil yokes, be yoked with your yoke, in the

name of Jesus.

133.   Any yoke that is eating up my sperms, break by fire, in the name of Jesus.

134.   Any yoke that is keeping me out of marriage, break to pieces, in the name of Jesus.

135.   Let the yoke that wants me to marry my enemy break by fire, in the name of Jesus.

136.   Every yoke of mental problems upon my life, break, in the name of Jesus.

137.   Every yoke of academic failures upon my life, break by fire, in the name of Jesus.

138.   Every yoke of personal madness upon my life, break, in the name of Jesus.

139.   You, African yoke of bondage upon my life, break now, in the name of Jesus.

140.   Any ritual yoke that was assigned to destroy my life, break, in the name of Jesus.

141.   Any yoke that was placed upon my life from the

womb, break to pieces, in the name of Jesus.

142.   Every witchcraft yoke upon my greatness, break, in the name of Jesus.

143.   Any power that wants to reduce me to temple altar girl or boy, die, in the name of Jesus.

144.   I break every evil yoke that is bringing distress into my life, in the name of Jesus.

145.   I break and loose myself from the yoke of grief and sorrow, in the name of Jesus

146.   Every abnormal increase in my life, disappear, in the name of Jesus.

147.   Any physical manifestation of evil load upon my life, die, in the name of Jesus.

148.   Let the spirit of paralysis living inside me die, in the name of Jesus.

149.   Any evil yoke that was assigned to waste my life, break, in the name of Jesus.

150.   Every chain of bondage upon my life, break, in the

name of Jesus.

151. Any power that is preventing me from doing good, die, in the name of Jesus.

152. Let evil powers that are wasting my efforts die by fire, in the name of Jesus.

153. Any power that has swallowed my respect, vomit it and die, in the name of Jesus.

154. Spirit of uncontrollable desires for immorality in my life, come out and die, in the name of Jesus.

155. Any power that has caged me in bondage, release me by fire, in the name of Jesus.

156. Any problem in my life that is stronger than my strength, die, in the name of Jesus.

157. Every moral weakness in my destiny, disappear, in the name of Jesus.

158. Every yoke of transgression upon my life, loose your hold, in the name of Jesus.

159. Any evil trap that was set for my life, catch fire, in

the name of Jesus.

160.   Any yoke of transgression that was assigned to disgrace my life, break to pieces, in the name of Jesus,

161.   Any power that is against my salvation, die, in the name of Jesus.

162.   I destroy that power limiting my spiritual life, in the name of Jesus.

163.   Blood of Jesus, sanctify me and keep me holy, in the name of Jesus.

164.   Father Lord, break every yoke of iniquity in my life, in the name of Jesus.

165.   Lord Jesus, deliver me from the yoke of transgression, in the name of Jesus.

166.   Every chain of transgression upon my life, break, in the name of Jesus.

167.   Anything in my life that is fighting against God, die, in the name of Jesus.

168. Every yoke of corruption and violence in my life, break, in the name of Jesus.

169. Any evil yoke that is dragging me back to Egypt, break to pieces, in the name of Jesus.

170. Any yoke that is linking me to any strange woman or man, break, in the name of Jesus.

171. Any yoke of immorality upon my life, break, in the name of Jesus.

172. Every Pentecostal witchcraft yoke upon my life, break, in the name of Jesus.

173. I break and loose my life from every yoke of satanic manipulation, in the name of Jesus.

174. Every yoke of love of money upon my life, break, in the name of Jesus.

175. Father Lord, break to pieces every yoke of pride in my life, in the name of Jesus.

176. Blood of Jesus, cleanse every evil mark upon my life, in the name of Jesus.   .

177. I destroy the evil yoke of the youth upon my life, in the name of Jesus.

178. Any yoke that is attacking my life because of my past sinful life, break by fire, in the name of Jesus.

179. You the yoke of my childhood, following me about, die forever, in the name of Jesus.

180. Any evil thing that took place during the time of my youth, die, in the name of Jesus.

181. Every activities of the household wickedness against my life, die, in the name of Jesus.

182. Every carnal yoke against my youth, disappear, in the name of Jesus.

183. Any yoke of deceit against my youth, break, in the name of Jesus.

184. Any spirit of rebellion against my youth, die, in the name of Jesus.

185. You my family yoke of sin, I am not your candidate leave me alone, in the name of Jesus.

186. Every yoke of foolishness upon my youth, break by fire, in the name of Jesus.

187. Oh Lord, break every evil yoke upon my life, in the name of Jesus.

188. Any seed of premature death upon my life, die, in the name of Jesus.

189. Fire of God, break every evil yoke upon my life, in the name of Jesus.

190. By your name called wonderful, I break every evil yoke upon my life, in the name of Jesus.

191. 1 decree destruction upon every yoke attacking my destiny, in the name of Jesus.

192. Every parental yoke upon my life, break, in the name of Jesus.

193. By the name of Jesus; I break to pieces every water spirit yoke in my life, in the name of Jesus.

194. Every humiliating yoke upon my life, break, in the name of Jesus.

195. O Lord, develop every undeveloped area of my life, in the name of Jesus.

196. Any power that initiates evil yoke, your time is up, die, in the name of Jesus.

197. Every yoke of bewitchment upon my life, be broken by fire, in the name of Jesus.

198. O deaths; death; kill every problem in my life, in the name of Jesus.

199. Every evil invitation given to Satan into my life, l withdraw you now, in the name of Jesus.

200. 1n the presence of God; I break every evil yoke working against my destiny, in the name of Jesus.

201. Every yoke of hatred upon my life, break, in the name of Jesus.

202. Jesus, take me away from every evil yoke, in the name of Jesus.

203. Lord Jesus, begin to set me free from every evil yoke, in the name of Jesus.

204.　　Any evil yoke holding my jaws, break and release me now, in the name of Jesus.

205.　　Any evil yoke, controlling my tongue, break by fire, in the name of Jesus.

206.　　Father Lord, bridle my tongue and control my utterances, in the name of Jesus.

207.　　I receive complete deliverance from the yoke of the jaws, in the name of Jesus.

208.　　Any evil yoke causing me to wrongly use my tongue, break to pieces, in the name of Jesus.

209.　　Let the evil yoke that closes my month when it supposed to open break, in the name of Jesus.

210.　　Father Lord; break the yoke using me to-talk indignantly against my helpers, in the name of Jesus.

211.　　Any power influencing me to scold people anyhow, die, in the name of Jesus.

212.　　Father Lord, prevent me from taking any evil

action, in the name of Jesus.

213. You spirit of deaf and dumb in my life; come out and die, in the name of Jesus.

214. You jaw yokes of dumbness in my life; your time is up, die, in the name of Jesus.

215. You thou yoke of deafness in my life, your time is up, die, in the name of Jesus.

216. O Lord, help me to make spiritual progress, in the name of Jesus.

217. Father Lord, cause me to hear what you are telling me, in the name of Jesus.

218. Blood of Jesus, help me to act rightly to the glory of God, in the name of Jesus.

219. 1 refuse to disobey my God, 1 will keep God's commandments, in the name of Jesus.

220. Any power, killing God things in my life, die, in the name of Jesus.

221. I refuse to disobey divine counsel, in the name of

Jesus.

222. Any yoke of jaws, leading me into rebellion, break, in the name of Jesus.

223. Let the yoke of jaws assigned to prevail over me die, in the name of Jesus.

224. Any evil yoke that wants to burry my destiny, break by fire, in the name of Jesus.

225. You that yoke that cleaved upon Gehazi, leave me alone and die, in the name of Jesus.

226. Every yoke of covetousness upon my life, break, in the name of Jesus.

227. You that jaw yoke upon my life, speaking against God, break, in the name of Jesus.

228. Every yoke of drunkenness upon my life, break, in the name of Jesus.

229. O Lord, use my mouth to say whatever you want to say, in the name of Jesus.

230. Let the evil yoke irritating my life break, in the

name of Jesus.

231.   Any occult personality using the yoke of jaw to manipulate my tongue, die, in the name of Jesus.

232.   O Lord, gives me victory over the human court, in the name of Jesus.

233.   1 refuse to obey any satanic command, in the name   of Jesus.

234.   Any power using evil yoke to control my life, break your yoke and die, in the name of Jesus.

235.   Any satanic yoke causing me to speak boastfully, break to pieces, in the name of Jesus.

236.   Any evil yoke spreading evil fire in the body of Christ, break by fire, in the name of Jesus.

237.   Let satanic power defiling the body of Christ be destroyed by fire, in the name of Jesus.

238.   Let the evil yoke assigned to confine me in a place break by fire, in the name of Jesus.

239.   Any witchcraft bird flying for my sake, die, in the name of Jesus.

240.   Any serpent of darkness ready to fight against my life, die, in the name of Jesus.

241.   Let the evil priest assigned to keep me under the yoke of Satan be disgraced, in the name of Jesus.

242.   Any evil yoke fashioned to time me for evil, break, in the name of Jesus.

243.   Father Lord, keep my tongue under your perfect control, in the name of Jesus.

244.   Any power making my tongue to speak unruly evil words, die, in the name of Jesus.

245.   Let all deadly poisonous word coming out of my mouth dry up, in the name of Jesus.

246.   O Lord, deliver me from cursing people you have blessed, in the name of Jesus.

247.   You my tongue, be controlled by God alone, in the name of Jesus.

248. Every satanic bondage upon my tongue, break by fire, in the name of Jesus.

249. O Lord, heal my tongue and prepare me for the rapture, in the name of Jesus.

250. O Lord, use my tongue to glorify your name, in the name of Jesus.

251. Any spirit of bitterness, envy and strife inside my heart, die, in the name of Jesus.

252. O Lord, help me to use my tongue in wisdom, in the name of Jesus.

253. Let the yoke of the jaw demanding for my life be broken, in the name of Jesus.

254. The daughter of Herodians shall not dance with my head, in the name of Jesus.

255. Any power assigned to cut off-my head, catch the fire of God, bums to ashes, in the name of Jesus.

256. You that power that bewitched John the Baptist, I am not your candidate, die, in the name of Jesus.

257. Let the witchcraft powers against my destiny be buried alive, in the name of Jesus.

258. Any evil yoke designed to waste my life, break, in the name of Jesus.

259. Let the witchcraft bungalows of my father's house collapse, in the name of Jesus.

260. Any yoke placed upon my Daniel in the lion's Den, break to pieces, in the name of Jesus.

261. O Lord, open my mouth in wisdom and your knowledge, in the name of Jesus.

262. Every yoke of bondage in my life, your time is up, break into pieces, in the name of Jesus

263. Every yoke of besetting sin upon my life, break, in the name of Jesus.

264. Oh Lord, help me to take firm decision like Enoch against sin, in the name of Jesus.

265. Every yoke of repenting and falling in my Life, break, in the name of Jesus.

266. Every yoke assigned to entangle me into evil powers, break, in the name of Jesus.

267. Every yoke of unbelief in my life, break by fire, in the name of Jesus.

268. Every yoke of unrighteousness in my life, break by fire, in the name of Jesus.

269. Every yoke of prostitution upon my life, break, in the name of Jesus.

270. Every yoke of wood upon my life, your time is up; break, in the name of Jesus.

271. Let all contagious yoke against my destiny break by fire, in the name of Jesus.

LET MY PHARAOH DIE

1.   O Lord, harden the heart of my Pharaoh for total destruction, in the name of Jesus.

2.   Let the boasting of my Pharaoh provoke my Lord to anger, in the name of Jesus.

3.   Let the cry of my afflicted destiny come to my God, in the name of Jesus.

4.   O God arise and let your anger be kindled with fire against my pharaoh, in the name of Jesus.

5.   Any Pharaoh challenging my God, fall down and die, in the name pf Jesus.

6.   O Lord arise and plagues my pharaoh and his agents, in the name of Jesus.

7.   Let my miracle of escape bring my Pharaoh unto the miracle of destruction, in the name of Jesus.

8.   Let the horse wheels of my pharaoh be dismantle, in the name of Jesus.

9. O Lord, with stands my Pharaoh's with pillar of fire, in the might in the name of Jesus.

10. O Lord, separates me from my Pharaoh's in the day with pillar of cloud, in the name of Jesus.

11. Any Pharaohs challenging my Moses, die, in the name of Jesus.

12. Any Pharaoh standing on my way to the promise land, die, in the name of Jesus.

13. Special announcement; Pharaoh, 1 am going to my promise land by force, in the name of Jesus.

14. O let my Pharaoh release all that you have taken from me, else your first son must die, in the name of Jesus.

15. O Lord, use my Moses as a trap against my Pharaoh, in the name of Jesus.

16. Let the dust turn against my Pharaohs, in the name of Jesus.

17. Let the servant of my Pharaoh turn against him, in the name of Jesus.

18. O Lord my God, arise and judge the god of my Pharaoh, in the name of Jesus.

19. Pharaoh! Pharaoh!! Pharaoh!!! let me go or else, you shall die, in the name of Jesus.

20. Any Pharaoh in my father's house, die, in the name of Jesus.

LET MY DESTINY ESCAPE BY FIRE

1.   Any power holding down my destiny to a spot, die, in the name of Jesus.

2.   You my destiny, what are you doing in witchcraft cage? Come out by fire, in the name of Jesus.

3.   Any power, cooking my destiny, break by fire, in the name of Jesus.

4.   Any satanic pot, cooking my destiny, break by fire, in the name of Jesus.

5.   Any power that has vowed to destroy my destiny, your time is up, therefore die, in the name of Jesus.

6.   Any satanic arrow fired against my destiny at any location, scatter by fire, in the name of Jesus.

7.   Every satanic gang up against my destiny at any location, scatter by fire, in the name of Jesus.

8.   I fire back, any dark arrow fired into my destiny, in the name of Jesus.

9.   I jump out from the cage of destiny destroyers, in the name of Jesus.

10.   You my destiny, become too hot for your enemies to handle, in the name of Jesus.

11.   O God my father, give me power to overcome destiny destroyers, in the name of Jesus.

12.   Fire of God, make a way of escape for me by fire, in the name of Jesus.

13.   Every satanic eye monitoring my destiny, receive double blindness, in the name of Jesus.

14.   Every satanic leg walking against my destiny, be paralyzed, in the name of Jesus.

15.   Every satanic hand holding my destiny, die, in the name of Jesus.

16.   O God of Abraham, Isaac and Jacob, remember my destiny by fire, in the name of Jesus.

17.   I refuse to cooperate below my destiny, in the name of Jesus.

18.   Whether my enemies like it or not, my destiny must shine, in the name of Jesus.

19.   You the Star of my destiny, arise and shine, in the name of Jesus.

20.   I cover my destiny with the blood of Jesus, in the name of Jesus.

I REFUSE TO BE DOMINATED

1. Any power struggling to make me the tail, die, in the name of Jesus.

2. You domineering spirit challenging my destiny, lose your hold and die, in the name of Jesus.

3. You the spirit of inferiority complex in my life, depart, in the name of Jesus.

4. Any power from my father's house, planning to put me under, die, in the name of Jesus.

5. Every satanic exchange of my right, scatter by fire, in the name of Jesus.

6. Every spirit of the tail pursuing after my destiny, fall down and die, in the name of Jesus.

7. Every serpent from my foundation dominating my life, release me and die, in the name of Jesus.

8. Every idol from my mother's house, dominating my destiny, catch fire, in the name of Jesus.

9.   Every idol from my mother's house, sitting on my dominions, be unseated by fire, in the name of Jesus.

10.   Thunder of God, strike down any satanic throne dominating my destiny, in the name of Jesus.

11.   I take authority over any strange man dominating my destiny, in the name of Jesus.

12.   Any powers from my foundation that controlled my father and now struggling to control me, die, in the name of Jesus.

13.   You my life, reject evil domineering spirit, in the name of Jesus.

14.   By fire by force 1 reject every evil domineering spirit, in the name of Jesus.

15.   Every satanic grip dominating my destiny, release me and die, in the name of Jesus.

16.   Every satanic influence over my life, die, in the name of Jesus.

17. I refuse to go by the direction of my enemies, in the name of Jesus.

18. By the power of God, I receive power to dominate, in the name of Jesus.

19. By the power of God, I receive power to speak and it comes to pass, in the name of Jesus.

20. Any power struggling with my destiny, die, in the name of Jesus.

MY EAGLE MUST FLY

1. Special announcement; powers of my father's house, whether, i must prosper, in the name of Jesus.

2. Every satanic nest prepared against my eagle, catch fire, in the name of Jesus.

3. Whether I like it or not, oh Lord, push me into my destiny, in the name of Jesus.

4. You my destiny, arise and shine, in the name of Jesus.

5. I must arise above those that started before me, in the name of Jesus.

6. O Lord, teach me to prosper above my fellows, in the name of Jesus.

7. Any evil arrow targeted against my eagle, backfire, in the name of Jesus.

8. You the eagle of my destiny, receive strength by fire, in the name of Jesus.

9.   Let my eagle fly above every satanic agent, in the name of Jesus.

10.   You the eagle of my destiny, receive anointing to remain above only, in the name of Jesus.

11.   You my eagle, carry me to the room of my break-throughs, in the name of Jesus.

12.   Any power pulling my eagle down, receive fire and die, in the name of Jesus.

13.   Any power from the grave, calling my eagle to come down, die by fire, in the name of Jesus.

14.   Any idol, crying against my eagle, die, in the name of Jesus.

15.   Any man or woman, cursing my eagle, be disgraced, in the name of Jesus.

16.   Every curse of automatic failure targeted against my eagle, back fire, in the name of Jesus.

17.   I lose my eagle from stagnancy, in the name of Jesus.

18.   Backwardness; my eagle is not your candidate, in the name of Jesus.

19.   O Lord, uphold my eagle from falling, in the name of Jesus.

20.   O Lord, let my eagle magnetize your blessing, in the name of Jesus.

21.   Curse be unto anyone that curse my eagle, in the name of Jesus.

22.   Any evil power trading in my soul, die, in the name of Jesus.

23.   Every satanic trade by better on my soul, die, in the name of Jesus.

24.   Soul traders release me and die, in the name of Jesus.

25.   O Lord, let there be confusion in the camp of satanic against soul traders, in the name of Jesus.

26.   Satanic agents, my soul is not for sale, in the name of Jesus.

27. Every chain of darkness targeted against my soul, break by fire, in the name of Jesus.

28. Arrow of darkness, you shall not prosper in my soul, in the name of Jesus.

29. Every gain made by satanic traders through my soul, disappear, in the name of Jesus.

30. Every satanic bank constructed by soul traders against my life, die, in the name of Jesus.

31. You my soul, refuse to cooperate with the soul traders, in the name of Jesus.

32. 1 fire back every arrow of darkness fired into my life, in the name of Jesus.

33. Every promise made by my parents affecting my soul, die by fire, in the name of Jesus.

34. Every legal right of soul trader against my destiny, scatter by fire, in the name of Jesus.

35. Wherever soul traders may call my name, thunders of God, answer them, in the name of Jesus.

36. Let my enemies replace me in the court of soul traders, in the name of Jesus.

37. Anything in my life, giving opportunity to the soul traders, die, in the name of Jesus.

38. Every satanic market established for my sake, catch fire, in the name of Jesus.

39. Every trader; trading on my soul, scatter by fire, in the name of Jesus.

40. Fire of God, separate me from soul trader, in the name of Jesus.

41. I cover my soul with the blood of Jesus, in the name of Jesus.

O LORD, TAKE AWAY MY BURDEN

1. Any problem that has vowed to die with me, die alone, in the name of Jesus.

2. Any problem in my life that has given me a name, vanish by fire, in the name of Jesus.

3. Anything in my life, killing me little by little, die, in the name of Jesus.

4. Lord Jesus, take my burden and give me your peace, in the name of Jesus.

5. Any self-imposed burdens in my life, come out and die, in the name of Jesus.

6. You satanic burden in my life, catch fire, in the name of Jesus.

7. You inherited burden in my life, die by fire, in the name of Jesus.

8. Every burden of sin and Satan upon my life, release me and die, in the name of Jesus.

9. Every periodic sickness in my life, come out and die, in the name of Jesus.

10. Every burden of hatred in my life, be wiped away by the blood of Jesus, in the name of Jesus.

11. Any problem making me cry, your time is up, vanish by fire, in the name of Jesus.

12. I shall not surrender to my enemies, in the name of Jesus.

13. Every satanic mountain standing against my destiny, disappear by fire, in the name of Jesus.

14. Thunder of God, dismantle every satanic burden in my life, in the name of Jesus.

15. I break and loose myself from every satanic bondage, in the name of Jesus.

16. You the root of my problem, die, in the name of Jesus.

17. Any force pushing me into satanic bondage, die, in the name of Jesus.

18. By fire by force, 1 refuse to obey Satan and his bondage, in the name of Jesus.

19. God of Elijah, deliver me from every satanic bondage, in the name of Jesus.

20. I receive the anointing to miss-carry satanic burden, in the name of Jesus.

EATERS OF FLESH AND DRINKERS OF BLOOD

1. Any power using my blood as wine and water, die, in the name of Jesus.

2. Any satanic bank constructed for my sake, catch fire, in the name of Jesus.

3. Every disease caused by Satan in my blood, die, in the name of Jesus.

4. Blood of Jesus, mingle with my blood for empowerment, in the name of Jesus.

5. You that power that feed on flesh, my flesh is not your candidate, therefore, die, in the name of Jesus.

6. I inject into my blood the blood of Jesus, in the name of Jesus.   .

7. You my blood, become too hot for your enemies to handle, in the name of Jesus.

8. Blood of Jesus, kill any satanic poison in my blood, in the name of Jesus.

9. Any satanic meeting organized to eat my flesh, scatter by fire, in the name of Jesus.

10. You my flesh, become poison for the witches and wizards, in the name of Jesus.

11. Any power from my father's house that want to donate me to witchcraft coven, you are a liar, therefore, donate yourself, in the name of Jesus.

12. Any satanic pot in my mother's' side, cooking my flesh, break by fire, in the name of Jesus.

13. I refuse to agree with eaters of flesh and drinkers of blood, in the name of Jesus.

14. Hammer of God, dismantle the teeth of eaters of flesh in my family, in the name of Jesus.

15. Any eaters of flesh and drinkers of blood that is after my life, fall down and die, in the name of Jesus.

16. You my blood in my former boy or girl friend working against my life, come out and die, in the name of Jesus.

17. You the blood of my former boy/girlfriend inside me, dry up, in the name of Jesus.

18. Anywhere blood is crying against my destiny, blood of Jesus, silence them, in the name of Jesus.

PRAYERS TO BREAK YOKE OF DISFAVOR

1. Every anointing of disfavor upon my life; dry up now by fire, in the name of Jesus.

2. Every mark of disfavor upon my life; be washed off my life by the blood of Jesus, in the name of Jesus.

3. You spirit of disfavor attached to my life; be detached and destroyed by fire, in the name of Jesus.

4. I soak my life in the divine favor of God, in the name of Jesus.

5. Let men and women of substance, wealth and valor everywhere, begin to show me favor and acceptance, in the name of Jesus.

6. Lord my God, label me with your divine favor, in the name of Jesus.

7. Any power swallowing the results of my prayers; fall down and die, in the name of Jesus.

8. Every curse of disfavor operating in my life; break by fire, in the name of Jesus.

9. Every evil magnet attracting disfavor into my life; be destroyed by fire, in the name of Jesus.

10. Garment of disfavor in my life; burn to ashes, in the name of Jesus.

11. Evil mask of disfavor; I remove you by fire, in the name of Jesus.

12. Lord, deliver me from the bondage of disfavor, in the name of Jesus.

13. Anointing to be favored, fall upon my divine helpers, in the name of Jesus.

14. I refuse to live a disfavored life, in the name of Jesus.

15. Any burial procession organized for me; be disbanded, in the name of Jesus.

16. Every seed of failure in my destiny; die, in the name of Jesus.

17. Every witchcraft broom sweeping away my goodness; be roasted, in the name of Jesus.

18. Evil River, flowing into my life; dry up by fire, in the name of Jesus.

19. My door of success; open by fire, in the name of Jesus!

20. Spirit of disfavor in my life and destiny; die, in the name of Jesus.

21. Arrow of disfavor, fired against me; backfire, in the name of Jesus.

22. Divine favor of God; overshadow disfavor in my life, in the name of Jesus.

23. Anything in my life that is attracting disfavor, die, in the name of Jesus.

24. Spirit of disfavor; I speak total destruction to you, in the name of Jesus.

25. Spirit of disfavor; locate your senders and work against them, in the name of Jesus.

26. Any power, projecting disfavor into my life; die, in the name of Jesus.

27. I bind and put to flight all spirits of discouragement, in the name of Jesus.

28. I break the backbone of any spirit of conspiracy and treachery working against me, in the name of Jesus.

29. Lord, hammer my matter into the mind of those who will help me, in the name of Jesus.

30. Any satanic root of disfavor; be uprooted by fire, in the name of Jesus.

31. Any power of hard luck in my life; die, in the name of Jesus.

32. Any cobweb of disfavor existing in my life; catch fire, in the name of Jesus.

33. By the anointing of God, I break and release myself from any yoke of disfavor, in the name of Jesus.

34.   Blood of Jesus; swallow every trace of disfavor in my life, in the name of Jesus.

35.   Lord, deliver me from any reproach, in the name of Jesus.

36.   Blood of Jesus; nullify every evil yoke of disfavor in my life, in the name of Jesus.

37.   Holy Ghost fire; encamp around me, in the name of Jesus.

38.   The favor of God and men; overwhelm my life, in the name of Jesus.

39.   I thank you Lord for your divine favor, in the name of Jesus.

PRAYERS TO BREAK THE YOKE OF
MINISTERIAL FAILURE

1. Blood of Jesus; go into the foundation of my calling and ministry and flush out all unwanted deposits from there, in the name of Jesus.

2. Foundational witchcraft embargo placed upon my ministry and calling; break and scatter by fire, in the name of Jesus.

3. Every evil family altar, crying against my ministry and calling; SHUT UP and die, in the name of Jesus.

4. Any family/village idol, challenging my ministry and calling; die, in the name of Jesus.

5. Any weakness and defects, affecting my ministry and calling; be melted away by Holy Ghost fire, in the name of Jesus.

6. Inherited evil character in my life, affecting my ministry and calling; die, in the name of Jesus.

7. Every darkness, covering the glory of my ministry; disappear by fire, in the name of Jesus.

8. Reproach designed to mess up my ministry and calling; burn to ashes, in the name of Jesus.

9. Every covenant of failure attached to my ministry and calling; die and release me by fire, in the name of Jesus.

10. Every satanic village/family strongman, challenging my ministry and calling; collapse and die suddenly now, in the name of Jesus.

11. All the curses from my parents' household pursuing my ministry and calling; die suddenly by fire now, in the name of Jesus.

12. Multiple barriers against my ministry; receive multiple clearance by the fire of God, in the name of Jesus.

13. All Egyptian carry-overs polluting my ministry; die, in the name of Jesus.

14. Any ancestral stool troubling my ministry, catch fire and burn to ashes, in the name of Jesus.

15. Anointing for explosion in my ministry; fall upon me now by fire, in the name of Jesus.

16. Lord, inject fire into my ministry, in the name of Jesus.

17. Advertise my ministry with signs and wonders, in the name of Jesus.

18. Poverty; die in my ministry and calling, in the name of Jesus.

19. Any evil dedication, affecting my ministry; break and scatter by fire, in the name of Jesus.

20. Every conscious and unconscious yoke of ministerial failure, disappear by fire, in the name of Jesus.

21. Every satanic arrow of failure fired against my ministry; backfire, in the name of Jesus.

22. Every architect of problems against my advancement; receive permanent termination, in the name of Jesus.

23. All spiritual wolves working against my ministry and calling; be paralyzed, in the name of Jesus.

24. Every curse of automatic failure in any department of my life; break, in the name of Jesus.

25. I bind and paralyze every strongman of failure in my ministry, in the name of Jesus.

26. I receive fire and move forward, in the name of Jesus.

27. Lord, open unto me your good treasures, in the name of Jesus.

28. Any curse operating in my ministry; die, in the name of Jesus.

29. God, redeem my soul from the powers of darkness, in the name of Jesus.

30. I refuse to fail in my ministerial calling, in the name of Jesus.

31. Every mark of ministerial failure upon me; thunder and fire of God, destroy it, in the name of Jesus.

32. I fire back every arrow of ministerial failure, in the name of Jesus.

33. My ministry; reject failure, in the name of Jesus.

34. Every seed of failure in my life; die, in the name of Jesus.

35. Every spiritual limitation to my success; disappear, in the name of Jesus.

36. Lord, let me not enter the trap of failure, in the name of Jesus.

37. Any power attacking my calling and ministry; die, in the name of Jesus.

38. Foundational power working against my calling; be destroyed, in the name of Jesus.

39.   Every door opened to the enemy of my calling; be closed, in the name of Jesus.

40.   Every anti-ministry arrow fired into my life; backfire, in the name of Jesus.

41.   Power to fight against ministerial failure; fall upon me now, in the name of Jesus.

42.   Every witchcraft altar speaking failure into my life; shut up and die, in the name of Jesus.

43.   I withdraw my ministry from the evil altar of the woman that sits upon the ministry of God's people, in the name of Jesus.

44.   Anointing to succeed in my ministry; possess me by fire, in the name of Jesus.

45.   Any agent of darkness that has vowed that my ministry will not excel; die, in the name of Jesus.

46.   Anything in me that is destroying my ministry; come out and die, in the name of Jesus.

47. Any arrow of ministerial failure released into my life; backfire, in the name of Jesus.

48. Any yoke of ministerial failure upon my life; break by fire, in the name of Jesus.

49. Lord, deliver me from the spirit of ministerial failure, in the name of Jesus.

50. As a minister of God, my ministry will not be amputated, in the name of Jesus.

51. I shall not be a cast away in the race of God's work, in the name of Jesus.

52. I am not an image of failure; the word of God in me is quickening my spirit to put failure behind me, in the name of Jesus.

53. I loose myself from the grip of borrowing and begging, in the name of Jesus.

54. I thank you Lord for the victory you have given me, in the name of Jesus.

PRAYERS TO BREAK YOKE OF SEXUAL IMMORALITY

1.   Every demon of sexual perversion that has ever entered me; come out with all your teeth and die instantly, in the name of Jesus.

2.   Every sexual sin holding me in bondage; die and release me by fire, in the name of Jesus.

3.   You the demon of sexual lust, planted in my sex organ; come out from there and die, in the name of Jesus.

4.   Every strange sperm that has ever entered my body; run out by fire, in the name of Jesus.

5.   Every sexual satanic deposit, inside my genital organ; be flushed out by fire, in the name of Jesus.

6.   Let evil bondage that was introduced into my sex organ and life through sexual immorality break and scatter by fire, in the name of Jesus.

7.   I claim perfect and permanent deliverance by fire, in the name of Jesus.

8.   Any power from the marine world promoting sexual immorality in the church; die, in the name of Jesus.

9.   Any power committing sexual immorality with me in the dream; die, in the name of Jesus.

10.   Any power polluting my spiritual life through sexual immorality; die, in the name of Jesus.

11.   Anointing to do exploits; fall upon my life now, in the name of Jesus.

12.   Anointing to excel in my ministry; fall upon my life now, in the name of Jesus.

13.   My eyes; refuse to cooperate with seduction, in the name of Jesus.

14.   My body; you must be used for God's purpose and plan, in the name of Jesus.

15. Any influence of sexual immorality upon my life; disappear, in the name of Jesus.

16. Any seed of sexual immorality in my life; catch fire and burn to ashes, in the name of Jesus.

17. Any yoke of sexual immorality upon my life; break by fire, in the name of Jesus.

18. Every witchcraft seed of immorality sowed in my foundation; die immediately, in the name of Jesus.

19. Let witchcraft dogs that are releasing lust into my life in my dream die, in the name of Jesus.

20. I set ablaze every witchcraft altar manipulating my life to commit sexual immorality, in the name of Jesus.

21. Inherited evil character of sexual immorality from my father's and mother's house; die, in the name of Jesus.

22. Every sin of sexual immorality; die, in the name of Jesus.

23. I break free from every spirit of sexual immorality, in the name of Jesus.

24. I cleanse myself from sexual pollution, in the name of Jesus.

25. Every demon of sexual immorality assigned to my life; be bound and die, in the name of Jesus.

26. I command every force or power of sexual immorality to come against themselves, in the name of Jesus.

27. I break the hold of any evil power over my life, in the name of Jesus.

28. Lord, deliver me from sexual power over my life, in the name of Jesus.

29. Seed of sexual perversion in my life; die, in the name of Jesus.

30. Arrows of sexual immorality; die instantly, in the name of Jesus.

31. Let sexual immoralities in my life perish, in the name of Jesus.

32. I cleanse myself from spiritual pollution with the blood of Jesus, in the name of Jesus.

33. Every evil yoke upon my life by the queen of heaven; break by fire, in the name of Jesus.

34. I release myself from every soul-tie connection to marine witchcraft, in the name of Jesus.

35. I reject every satanic dream in any area of my life, in the name of Jesus.

36. Any foundational problem against my life; be broken by fire, in the name of Jesus.

37. Thank you, my Lord for answered prayers, in the name of Jesus.

PRAYERS TO BREAK THE YOKE OF MARITAL BREAK UP

1. Every yoke of marital break-up put upon my neck; I break you up by fire, in the name of Jesus.

2. Every arrow of marital failure and break-up ever fired into my life; jump out and burn to ashes, in the name of Jesus.

3. Any anti-marriage forces, working against my marriage; scatter by fire in the name of Jesus.

4. Every spiritual dowry, working against my marriage; catch fire and bum to ashes in the name of Jesus.

5. Any power that does not want me to enjoy my marital life; die, in the name of Jesus.

6. Every agent of marital destruction; pack out by fire, in the name of Jesus.

7. Holy Spirit, establish the kingdom of God in my marriage by fire, in the name of Jesus.

8.   Every architect of conflict and hostility in my home; be paralyzed, in the name of Jesus.

9.   Any power that is trying to redraw the map of my marriage, I put you to shame, in the name of Jesus.

10. I withdraw my marriage from the hands of evil designers, in the name of Jesus.

11. Satan, hear the word of the Living God; you will not break my marriage, in the name of Jesus.

12. Every evil imagination, thoughts, plan, decision, desire and expectation of divorce and separation against my home; be nullified, in the name of Jesus.

13. I plead the blood of Jesus over my body, soul and spirit, in the name of Jesus.

14. Every evil decision taken against my marriage in the witchcraft meeting; be cancelled by the blood of Jesus, in the name of Jesus.

15. You spirit husband/wife signing any marriage certificate; thunderbolt of God, destroy you, in the name of Jesus.

16. I announce to the heavens that Jesus is my husband/wife, in the name of Jesus.

17. Every spiritual weapon fashioned against my marriage, roast by fire, in the name of Jesus.

18. I cancel any satanic influence on my marriage, in the name of Jesus.

19. Blood of Jesus restore and reconcile my marriage, in the name of Jesus.

20. I am the child of God; therefore, any power responsible for my marriage breakages; I am not your candidate, therefore, die, in the name of Jesus.

21. Any evil power that has vowed to break my marriage; die, in the name of Jesus.

22. Let the power trying to withdraw my marriage map be put to death in the name of Jesus.

23. Let all household wickedness release my marriage and die, in the name of Jesus.

24. I break the evil hold of the spirit husband/wife over my marriage, in the name of Jesus.

25. Lord, visit my marriage with your fire, in the name of Jesus.

26. Arrows of marital break-up, burn to ashes, in the name of Jesus.

27. I refuse evil counsel that may bring about marital break-up in my life, in the name of Jesus.

28. My marriage; be too hot for any marital break-up arrow to prosper in the name of Jesus.

29. Every architect of conflict, die, in the name of Jesus.

30. I deliver my marriage from the hands of home wreckers, in the name of Jesus.

31. Satan, hear the word of the Lord; you will not break my marriage, in the name of Jesus.

32. I pursue, overtake and recover my marriage from the hands of marriage breakers, in the name of Jesus.

33. Lord, dissolve and render to naught every evil counsel and fashioned against my home, in the name of Jesus.

34. I refuse to be a second-hand wife or married single lady, in the name of Jesus.

35. I deliver my husband/wife from the hand of evil seducers, in the name of Jesus.

36. Evil pattern of marital break-up in this end time, I am not your candidate; therefore, depart from me, in the name of Jesus.

37. You that strange woman behind marital break-up; your time is up; therefore, die, in the name of Jesus.

38. Holy Spirit, reverse the pace at which marriages are attacked these days, in the name of Jesus.

39.   I rededicate my marriage to you Lord, in the name of Jesus.

40.   Every anti-marriage altar speaking death and break- up to my marriage; catch fire, in the name of Jesus.

41.   Any power that is hindering my marital peace; die, in the name of Jesus.

42.   Any strange fire that exists in my marriage; disappear by fire, in the name of Jesus.

43.   I thank you Lord for saving my marriage in the name of Jesus.

PRAYERS TO BREAK THE YOKE OF DRUNKENNESS

1. Every evil spirit of drunkenness, planted in my taste bud; be uprooted and cast out by fire, in the name of Jesus.

2. Every anointing that is activating drunkenness in my life, dry up and die, in the name of Jesus.

3. Let witchcraft powers that are behind addiction to alcohol in my life be roasted by fire, in the name of Jesus.

4. Every spell of drunkenness casted against me; I neutralize you by the blood of Jesus, in the name of Jesus.

5. Holy Ghost fire; kill every desire, appetite and lust for alcohol in my heart and spirit in the name of Jesus.

6. I command total and complete deliverance from every yoke of drunkenness in my life, in the name of Jesus.

7. Every yoke of drunkenness upon my life; break, in the name of Jesus.

8. Every curse of parental addiction to alcohol in my life; break, in the name of Jesus.

9. I refuse to be called a drunkard, in the name of Jesus.

10. You unfriendly friends manipulating my life; die, in the name of Jesus.

11. Every environmental influence upon my life; be nullified, in the name of Jesus.

12. By the power of God, I destroy every spirit of drunkenness that is ruling in my life, in the name of Jesus.

13. Arrow of drunkenness released into my life; backfire, in the name of Jesus.

14.   Any evil influence of drunkenness upon my life; disappear, in the name of Jesus.

15.   Any personality that is suppressing my will to overcome drunkenness; die, in the name of Jesus.

16.   Every curse of drunkenness threatening my destiny; break by fire, in the name of Jesus.

17.   Blood of Jesus, fight every spirit of drunkenness in my life, in the name of Jesus.

18.   18.   Blood of Jesus, speak death to every evil appetite for alcohol in my life, in the name of Jesus.

19.   I take back my life from every evil altar of drunkenness, in the name of Jesus.

20.   Blood of Jesus, deliver me from the powers of drunkenness, in the name of Jesus.

21.   Any witchcraft pot in my stomach; break in the name of Jesus.

22.   Holy Ghost fire, possess every department of my life, in the name of Jesus.

23.   Inherited spirit of alcohol; die, in the name of Jesus

24.   Lord, deliver me by fire, in the name of Jesus.

25.   I decree instant death to the spirit of drunkenness, in the name of Jesus.

26.   Any evil river flowing in my life; dry up, in the name of Jesus.

27.   Lord, visit my foundation by fire, in the name of Jesus.

28.   I bind the spirit of negative destiny in my life, in the name of Jesus.

29.   Let the fire of God saturate my life, in the name of Jesus.

30.   I reject all evil manipulation and manipulators, in the name of Jesus.

31. Lord, let me drink your blood when I am thirsty for alcohol, in the name of Jesus.

32. I release myself from any spirit of addiction, in the name of Jesus.

33. Blood of Jesus, quench my taste for alcohol/ in the name of Jesus.

34. Blood of Jesus, nullify every generational curse against me in the name of Jesus.

35. Every evil yoke attached to this curse; break by fire, in the name of Jesus.

36. I break the soul-tie with unfriendly friends in the name of Jesus.

37. I thank you Lord for delivering me, in the name of Jesus.

PRAYERS TO BREAK YOKE OF INIQUITY

1.   Every yoke of iniquity deeply rooted in my soul, spirit and body; what are you waiting for? Die by fire, in the name of Jesus.

2.   Let every stronghold of iniquity in my blood be destroyed by the blood of Jesus, in the name of Jesus.

3.   The demon behind sin in my life; die, in the name of Jesus.

4.   Let the root and seed of sin die suddenly in my heart, in the name of Jesus.

5.   Let the blood of Jesus mixed with the fire of God penetrate my heart with force and knock out iniquity from my heart completely, in the name of Jesus.

6.   Every tree of iniquity planted in my foundation; be uprooted by fire, in the name of Jesus.

7.   Iniquity shall not be my portion, in the name of Jesus.

8. Let my spirit man receive spiritual cleansing, in the name of Jesus.

9. I release myself from ancestral and demonic pollution, in the name of Jesus.

10. You the throne of iniquity operating in my life; die, in the name of Jesus.

11. Every generational curse of God resulting from the sins of idolatry on my forefathers; lose your hold in the name of Jesus.

12. Every ancestral placenta manipulation in my life; be reversed, in the name of Jesus.

13. Evil ancestral life pattern, die in the name of Jesus.

14. My life, be washed by the blood of Jesus, in the name of Jesus.

15. Any iniquity in my life, Holy Spirit; wash it away, in the name of Jesus.

16. Any iniquity in my life; receive the fire of God today, in the name of Jesus.

17.   Iniquity; your time is up in my life; therefore, I depart by force, in the name of Jesus.

18.   Holy Ghost fire, swallow every iniquity in my life now, in the name of Jesus.

19.   Thou yoke of iniquity in my life, break to pieces, in the name of Jesus.

20.   Mark of iniquity; be wiped off by the blood of Jesus, in the name of Jesus.

21.   Throne of iniquity; scatter, in the name of Jesus.

22.   Lord, deliver me by fire, in the name of Jesus.

23.   By the blood of Jesus, I come out from iniquity, in the name of Jesus.

24.   Failure shall not slaughter my destiny, in the name of Jesus.

25.   I withdraw every mandate given to any evil power to supervise my life, in the name of Jesus.

26.   Every evil deposit from the sun against my life; the Lord rebuke you, in the name of Jesus.

27.   You hidden arrow of wickedness; come out by fire, in the name of Jesus.

28.   I disgrace every altar of iniquity in my life by the blood of Jesus, in the name of Jesus.

29.   Every evil programmed into my foundation; die, in the name of Jess.

30.   Lord, separate me from the iniquity of my ancestors, in the name of Jesus.

31.   Every evil seed of iniquity in my life; perish, in the name of Jesus.

32.   Every root of iniquity that is eating up my life little by little, die, in the name of Jesus.

33. Any growth of iniquity in my life; catch fire and burn to ashes, in the name of Jesus.

34. Any evil imagination in my heart; vanish, in the name of Jesus.

35. Any power that is reviving iniquity in my life; die, in the name of Jesus.

36. Any arrow of iniquity that has been released into my life; backfire, in the name of Jesus.

37. I confess all known and unknown sins of my ancestors, in the name of Jesus.

38. I plead the blood of Jesus over my sins, in the name of Jesus.

39. I depart from iniquity of my family life, in the name of Jesus.

40. I soak my life in the blood of Jesus, in the name of Jesus.

41. Power of God, fall upon my life; in the name of Jesus.

42.   Lord, I thank you for delivering me from my iniquities, in the name of Jesus.

PRAYERS TO BREAK YOKE OF BAD HABITS

1.   Every evil habit in my life and foundation; die, in the name of Jesus.

2.   Every yoke of evil habit in my life; be broken by fire, in the name of Jesus.

3.   Let every inherited evil habit be destroyed completely from my life now, in the name of Jesus.

4.   Let the consuming fire of God dig deep into my life and kill all the evil habits out of my life, in the name of Jesus.

5.   Let the blood of Jesus enter my roots and purge my evil habits out of me, in the name of Jesus.

6. Blood of Jesus, poison every evil habit in my life to death, in the name of Jesus.

7. Any character in me that does not portray God's own; die, in the name of Jesus.

8. Lord, inject into my life the character of Jesus Christ, in the name of Jesus.

9. Let the excellent character of Jesus Christ be transfused in my life, in the name of Jesus.

10. Every desire of the enemy for my life shall not prosper, in the name of Jesus.

11. Every spirit of destruction, release me by fire, in the name of Jesus.

12. Any strongman sitting on the throne of my life; be unseated and die, in the name of Jesus.

13. Any power promoting bad habits in my life, die, in the name of Jesus.

14. Lord my God, lead me into the path of righteousness, in the name of Jesus.

15.   You my life, change by fire, in the name of Jesus.

16.   Inherited bad habit; die, in the name of Jesus.

17.   Anointing that destroys yoke of bad habits; fall upon me in the name of Jesus.

18.   Power of God's deliverance; fall upon me, in the name of Jesus.

19.   Every yoke of bad habits; break by fire, by force, in the name of Jesus.

20.   Spirit of bad habits, I command you to die a permanent death/ in the name of Jesus.

21.   Blood of Jesus; flush out every bad habit in my life, in the name of Jesus.

22.   Every reoccurrence of bad habits; stop by fire, in the name of Jesus.

23.   Anointing of bad habit in my life; dry up, in the name of Jesus

24.   Any evil personality introducing evil habit into my life; die, in the name of Jesus.

25. You my life; reject bad habit, in the name of Jesus.

26. Stubborn bad habit pulling me away from serving my God whole-heartedly; die immediately, in the name of Jesus.

27. Holy Spirit, help me to crucify flesh, in the name of Jesus.

28. I deliver myself from the spirit of stealing, in the name of Jesus

29. I refuse to be a liar, in the name of Jesus

30. Lord, help me to develop and manifest the fruit of the spirit, in the name of Jesus.

31. Every root of bad habit in my life; catch fire and burn to ashes, in the name of Jesus.

32. Any habit of a beast that is manifesting in my life; come out and die, in the name of Jesus.

33. Any evil personality that is in control of my character; die, in the name of Jesus.

34. Anything in me that is making me not to be behaving well; come out by fire, in the name of Jesus.

35. I release myself from any ungodly power, in the name of Jesus.

36. Any evil corruptible power; break and release me, in the name of Jesus.

37. I cut off every evil soul-tie, in the name of Jesus.

38. I break and loose myself from evil yoke by fire, in the name of Jesus.

39. I come against evil habits from my paternal and maternal houses, and I command you to die by fire, in the name of Jesus.

40. You the strongman in my father's and mother's house; wherever you are; die, in the name of Jesus.

41. I thank you God for answered prayers, in the name of Jesus.

PRAYERS TO BREAK YOKE OF WITCHCRAFT

1.   Every chain of witchcraft put upon my neck; I break and destroy you by fire, in the name of Jesus.

2.   Any witchcraft load placed upon my head; I shake and cast you off into the fire of destruction, in the name of Jesus.

3.   Every witchcraft stronghold, tormenting my life; be dismantled and destroyed by the bulldozers of the Lord, in the name of Jesus.

4.   Every witchcraft material circulating in my body; be flushed and pushed out by fire, in the name of Jesus.

5.   Let every ministry of witchcraft, their altar and instruments, receive fire and burn to ashes, in the name of Jesus.

6.   Every witchcraft powerhouse working against me; receive bomb blast from heaven and scatter by fire, in the name of Jesus.

7. All witchcraft thrones, seats, gadgets, and ministry, working against me, receive fire and burn to ashes, in the name of Jesus.

8. Any witch or wizard that receives mandate from Satan to attack me; receive brain damage; run mad and die, in the name of Jesus.

9. I withdraw my name, soul, spirit and body from every witchcraft register, in the name of Jesus.

10. Let all witchcraft agenda, missions and plans against me be completely frustrated, in the name of Jesus.

11. Every damage done to my life through witchcraft; be reversed, cancelled, and be repaired by fire, in the name of Jesus.

12. Any witchcraft altar in my foundation; catch fire, in the name of Jesus.

13. I receive power against household witchcraft, in the name of Jesus.

14. Any power from the kingdom of marine witchcraft in charge of my life; die, in the name of Jesus.

15. Let the thunder of God locate and dismantle the throne of witchcraft in my household, in the name of Jesus.

16. Thunder of God; scatter beyond redemption every foundation of witchcraft in my household, in the name of Jesus.

17. Any yoke of witchcraft upon my life; break by fire, in the name of Jesus.

18. I plead the blood of Jesus on my body, soul and spirit, in the name of Jesus.

19. Holy Ghost fire; ignite my spirit with your fire, in the name of Jesus.

20. Power of the living God let your word stand in my life, in the name of Jesus.

21. Any witchcraft power that is fighting to control my life, receive destruction, in the name of Jesus.

22.   Any of my possession in the hands of witchcraft power; be restored to me by fire, in the name of Jesus.

23.   I damage the brain of that witch that is planning to pull me down, in the name of Jesus.

24.   Blood of Jesus; swallow any witchcraft power that is fighting to swallow my destiny, in the name of Jesus.

25.   Any witch that attacks me before; I render you powerless, in the name of Jesus.

26.   Every witchcraft curse targeted at me; break, in the name of Jesus.

27.   Any witchcraft power that wants to waste my destiny; die, in the name of Jesus.

28.   You that mistress of witchcraft in my family; what are you waiting for? Die, in the name of Jesus.

29.   Any witchcraft power that is sitting upon my money, fall down and die, in the name of Jesus.

30. Every stubborn witchcraft power that has vowed to divert my destiny; receive the judgment fire of God, in the name of Jesus.

31. Witchcraft curse attacking my life; break by the power in the blood of Jesus, in the name of Jesus.

32. I refuse to be destroyed by any witch or wizard harassing my life, in the name of Jesus.

33. Every witchcraft manipulation upon my life; cease by fire, in the name of Jesus.

34. Spirit of witchcraft; cease to operate in my life from today, in the name of Jesus.

35. Inherited witchcraft yoke; break, in the name of Jesus.

36. Ancestral witchcraft yoke; break, in the name of Jesus.

37. Anything in my life cooperating with witchcraft; die, in the name of Jesus.

38. I receive power against witchcraft, in the name of Jesus

39. Every witchcraft coven designed for my sake; O God; scatter them by fire, in the name of Jesus.

40. Any decision taken against me in any witchcraft meeting; be destroyed by fire, in the name of Jesus.

41. Let the thunder and fire of God locate any witchcraft meeting against my life, and destroy them by fire, in the name of Jesus.

42. I release myself and break any evil yoke placed upon me by witchcraft agents, in the name of Jesus.

43. I thank you Father for giving me the power over witchcraft spirit, in the name of Jesus.

PRAYERS TO BREAK YOKE OF EVIL INHERITANCE

1. Every rope of evil binding me down in bondage; burn to ashes, in the name of Jesus.

2. Every inherited sickness and disease from my parents; die by fire, in the name of Jesus.

3. Every evil family pattern flowing into my life; die by fire, in the name of Jesus.

4. Every evil flow into my life; be terminated by fire, in the name of Jesus.

5. Every garment of tribulation and sorrow passed over to me as inheritance; burn to ashes, in the name of Jesus.

6. Inherited poverty in my life die; in the name of Jesus.

7. All inherited curses, evil covenants, sicknesses and diseases in my life; quench by fire, in the name of Jesus.

8. I refuse to inherit any evil inheritance, in the name of Jesus.

9. I break and loose myself from any inherited evil covenant, in the name of Jesus.

10. Blood of Jesus; flush out from my system every inherited satanic deposit, in the name of Jesus.

11. I release myself from the grip of any problem transferred into my life from the womb, in the name of Jesus.

12. I command all foundational strongman attached to my life to be paralyzed, in the name of Jesus.

13. Any property of Satan in my possession; die in the name of Jesus.

14. I disentangle myself from evil inheritance, in the name of Jesus.

15. Evil inheritance of affliction; die, in the name of Jesus.

16. Evil inheritance of slavery; die, in the name of Jesus.

17. Yoke of inherited problems; break, in the name of Jesus.

18. Yoke of evil inheritance; break, in the name of Jesus.

19. I break away from every yoke of evil inheritance, in the name of Jesus.

20. Father Lord, repair any damage done to my life by this evil inheritance, in the name of Jesus.

21. Every foundational evil inheritance polluting my destiny; lose your hold over my life, in the name of Jesus.

22. I reject evil inheritance from my ancestors, in the name of Jesus.

23. Bondage of evil inheritance; break and release me, in the name of Jesus.

24. Lord, release all my divine inheritance, in the name of Jesus.

25. Distributor of evil inheritance in my life; die, in the name of Jesus.

26. I release myself from evil foundational bondage that I inherited, in the name of Jesus.

27. Yoke of evil inheritance; break by fire, in the name of Jesus.

28. Any evil inheritance that I have inherited from my past mistakes of evil; be destroyed by fire, in the name of Jesus

29. Lord, send your axe to the foundation of my life, in the name of Jesus.

30. Blood of Jesus, flush out every evil inheritance in my life, in the name of Jesus.

31. Blood of Jesus, purge me from any satanic deposit as a result of evil inheritance, in the name of Jesus.

32. You evil hand placed on my head when I was a child; wither, in the name of Jesus.

33. Lord, let your creative power operate afresh in my life, in the name of Jesus.

34. Thank you, Lord, in the name of Jesus.

PRAYERS TO BREAK YOKE OF RISING AND FALLING

1. You the yoke of rising and falling; break and release my life by fire, in the name of Jesus.

2. Every weakness in my spiritual life; die, in the name of Jesus.

3. Holy Ghost fire, boil out every contamination from my life, in the name of Jesus.

4. Holy Spirit, inject power into my spiritual muscles by fire, in the name of Jesus.

5. Power to stand firmly and rooted deeply in the Rock of Ages; fall upon me, in the name of Jesus.

6. Special announcement: Satan when I fall seven times, I shall arise seven times, in the name of Jesus!

7. Every spirit of backwardness controlling my life; die, in the name of Jesus.

8.   Any power that does not want my life to move forward; die by fire, in the name of Jesus.

9.   You the eagle of my life; rise up by fire, in the name of Jesus.

10.   Every curse of rising and falling in my foundation; break, in the name of Jesus.

11.   Jesus is Lord over my body soul and spirit; therefore; when I fall, I shall rise, in the name of Jesus.

12.   Lord, let your light shine on me, in the name of Jesus.

13.   Holy Ghost, arise and let my enemies be scattered, in the name of Jesus.

14.   I reverse any evil pronouncement issued against me, in the name of Jesus.

15.   Every evil yoke upon my life; break into irreparable pieces, in the name of Jesus.

16. Resurrection power of God; fall upon my life, in the name of Jesus.

17. I shall arise and shine, in the name of Jesus.

18. Affliction shall not rise up for the second time, in the name of Jesus.

19. Any spirit of rising and falling upon my life; die, in the name of Jesus.

20. Any arrow of rising and falling released into my life; break by fire, in the name of Jesus.

21. Any evil influence of rising and falling upon my life; disappear, in the name of Jesus.

22. Any power of unstableness in my life; die, in the name of Jesus.

23. I break every spirit of rising and falling in my life, in the name of Jesus.

24. I refuse to be a rising and falling Christian, in the name of Jesus.

25.   You that spirit of rising and falling; I command you to lose your hold over my life, in the name of Jesus.

26.   Wicked anointing of rising and falling; be flushed out of my system, in the name of Jesus.

27.   Every source of a life of rising and falling; be cut off, in the name of Jesus.

28.   I shall rise and never fall again, in the name of Jesus.

29.   I bind and cast you out of my life forever, in the name of Jesus.

30.   Any evil remote controlling power; die, in the name of Jesus.

31.   Spirit of backsliding in my life; die, in the name of Jesus.

32.   Lord, keep me standing by your power, in the name of Jesus.

33.   Arrow of demotion; backfire in the name of Jesus.

34.   Thank you, Lord, in the name of Jesus.

PRAYERS TO BREAK YOKE OF
ENVIRONMENTAL FORCES

1.   Every environmental force tormenting my life; die, in the name of Jesus.

2.   Every territorial strongman in charge of my case; die suddenly by fire, in the name of Jesus.

3.   Every network of environmental powers, working hard to pull me down; catch fire and burn to ashes, in the name of Jesus.

4.   The power controlling my environment; fall down and die, in the name of Jesus.

5.   Every damage done to my life by environmental forces; be reversed by fire in the name of Jesus.

6.   Let any decision, conclusion, decree and declaration of powers from my environment be nullified in the name of Jesus.

7. Environmental strongman in charge of my life; release me and let me go in the name of Jesus.

8. Any power from my environment that says I shall not make it; you are a liar; therefore, die in the name of Jesus.

9. Spirit of the Living God, take absolute control over my environment, in the name of Jesus.

10. I refuse to be limited, in the name of Jesus.

11. Environmental curse; break, in the name of Jesus.

12. Environmental bondage; break, in the name of Jesus.

13. Any environmental power controlling me; die, in the name of Jesus.

14. I receive power to break environmental yokes, in the name of Jesus.

15. Every yoke of environmental forces in my abode; lose your hold over my life, in the name of Jesus.

16.   Environmental bondage; I render you useless in my life, in the name of Jesus.

17.   Every environmental force working against my destiny; die instant death, in the name of Jesus.

18.   Environmental forces; begin to work against your agents, in the name of Jesus.

19.   Every environmental yoke affecting my life; break by fire, in the name of Jesus.

20.   Every environmental power, holding me bound in this vicinity; break by thunder, in the name of Jesus.

21.   Lord, rebuke every environmental strongman monitoring my progress, in the name of Jesus.

22.   I release myself from environmental bondage, in the name of Jesus.

23.   Satanic elders, sponsoring environmental yokes in the lives of the youth in my family; receive judgment by fire, in the name of Jesus.

24.   Any environmental power attacking me; receive arrows of life, in the name of Jesus.

25.   Let my environment refuse to listen to the voice of my enemies, in the name of Jesus.

26.   Let my environment become too hot for demons to occupy, in the name of Jesus.

27.   Holy Ghost fire, saturate my environment and produce testimonies, in the name of Jesus.

28.   Every environmental stronghold and satanic structure; scatter, in the name of Jesus.

29.   Any environmental power operating in my environment; die, in the name of Jesus.

30.   Any evil altar that is in my environment; catch fire and burn to ashes, in the name of Jesus.

31.   Any environmental power limiting the life of the youth in my environment; enough is enough; therefore, die, in the name of Jesus.

32. Lord, deliver me from any evil pollution, in the name of Jesus.

33. Blood of Jesus, purge me from any evil contamination, in the name of Jesus.

34. Fire of God; consume any environmental power in the name of Jesus.

35. You stubborn enemies in my environment; die, in the name of Jesus.

36. Thank you, Father, in the name of Jesus.

PRAYERS TO BREAK YOKE OF SLEEPLESSNESS

1.   You the yoke of sleeplessness upon my neck; break and scatter by fire, in the name of Jesus.

2.   Anything that does not allow me to sleep well, die, in the name of Jesus.

3.   You the demon behind sleeplessness in my life; die, suddenly by fire, in the name of Jesus.

4.   Any power preventing me from enjoying my sleep; die suddenly, in the name of Jesus.

5.   Early unprofitable waking up; die in my life by fire, in the name of Jesus.

6.   Every emotional strain, nightmare, anxiety and depression, causing sleeplessness in my life; die suddenly by fire, in the name of Jesus.

7.   Any problem causing sleeplessness in my life; disappear, in the name of Jesus.

8.   I paralyze all problem expanders, in the name of Jesus.

9. I lose myself from satanic bondage, in the name of Jesus.

10. I lose myself from any power of witchcraft, in the name of Jesus.

11. I claim sound and refreshing sleep by fire, in the name of Jesus.

12. I claim safety from all perils of the night, in the name of Jesus.

13. I claim freedom from satanic powers and restless dreams, in the name of Jesus.

14. I commit my body, soul and spirit to your care, O Father, as I sleep in the name of Jesus.

15. Father, let me experience the brightness of Thy presence, in the name of Jesus.

16. Power of sleeplessness in my life; die, in the name of Jesus.

17. Power of God; break every stubborn yoke of sleeplessness in my life in the name of Jesus.

18. Every spirit of sleeplessness in my system; be flushed out of my foundation, in the name of Jesus.

19. Evil pattern of sleeplessness; break in the name of Jesus

20. Satanic agent of sleeplessness; depart from me by fire, in the name of Jesus.

21. Sleeplessness; vanish from me, in the name of Jesus.

22. Power of sleeplessness; I command you to disappear from me, in the name of Jesus

23. Sleeplessness; receive confusion, in the name of Jesus.

24. Lord, deliver me from the spirit of sleeplessness, in the name of Jesus.

25. Power of sound sleep; fall upon me, in the name of Jesus.

26. Arrows of sleeplessness; backfire, in the name of Jesus.

27. Curse and enchantment against my sleep; break, in the name of Jesus.

28. I receive power to break yoke of sleeplessness, in the name of Jesus.

29. Any habit of sleeping too much that has taken over my life; die, in the name of Jesus.

30. Anointing to defeat the power of sleeplessness; overtake my life, in the name of Jesus.

31. Any witchcraft pot cooking my blood; break by fire, in the name of Jesus.

32. All wandering spirits in my mind, die, in the name of Jesus.

33. Every harassment of witches and wizard over my sleep; die, in the name of Jesus.

34. I refuse to rely on drugs before I sleep in the name of Jesus.

35. Lord, let your dew from heaven fall upon me, in the name of Jesus.

36. Thank you, Lord, in the name of Jesus.

PRAYERS TO BREAK YOKE OF INFIRMITIES

1. Every altar of infirmities in my life; catch fire and burn to ashes, in the name of Jesus.

2. Every force of witchcraft behind any infirmities in my body; be roasted by fire, in the name of Jesus.

3. The power feeding infirmities in my body; die suddenly by fire, in the name of Jesus.

4. I break and release myself from the stronghold of infirmities, in the name of Jesus.

5. Powers from hell, sponsoring infirmities in my body; die by fire, in the name of Jesus.

6. Let every satanic plantation of infirmities in my body; die suddenly, in the name of Jesus.

7. Every curse of infirmity upon my life; break by fire, in the name of Jesus.

8. Every spirit hindering my perfect healing; die, in the name of Jesus.

9.   Every knee of infirmity in my life; bow out, in the name of Jesus.

10.   Let the divine whirlwind scatter every vessel of infirmity fashioned against my life, in the name of Jesus.

11.   I rebuke every refuge of sickness, in the name of Jesus.

12.   Every inherited infirmity in my family; die, in the name of Jesus.

13.   Evil label of infirmity on my body; be wiped away by the blood of Jesus, in the name of Jesus.

14.   Infirmity that has turned itself into evil garment in my family, be roasted by fire, in the name of Jesus.

15.   Lord, turn my weakness into divine strength, in the name of Jesus.

16.   Any yoke of infirmities upon my life; break by fire, in the name of Jesus.

17. Any power that has kept me buried in infirmities; die, in the name of Jesus.

18. Any seed of infirmities in my life; catch fire, in the name of Jesus.

19. Anointing to destroy infirmities; possess me now, in the name of Jesus.

20. Any evil attachment between infirmities and me, receive fire and be destroyed, in the name of Jesus.

21. I release myself from every inherited sickness, in the name of Jesus.

22. I renounce any covenant of infirmities in my life, in the name of Jesus.

23. I fire back every arrow of infirmity, in the name of Jesus.

24. I claim divine health, in the name of Jesus.

25. Lord, perform the necessary surgical operation that would make me whole, in the name of Jesus.

26. Every infirmity in me; die, in the name of Jesus.

27. Infirmities; go back to sender, in the name of Jesus.

28. Lord, make my body a no-go area for any infirmities, in the name of Jesus.

29. Witchcraft arrow of infirmity fired into my life; backfire, in the name of Jesus.

30. Every agent of infirmity following me from place to place; die, in the name of Jesus.

31. Stubborn yoke of infirmity threatening my life; break immediately, in the name of Jesus.

32. Inherited yoke of infirmity; be destroyed by the blood of Jesus Christ, in the name of Jesus.

33. Anointing that destroys yokes; attack every root of infirmity, in the name of Jesus.

34. I lose and release myself from the curse of infirmity, in the name of Jesus.

35. Lord, let the power of the Holy Ghost overshadow me, in the name of Jesus.

36. I fire back every infirmity back to sender, in the name of Jesus.

37. My body will not be used as transport vehicles to demonic meeting, in the name of Jesus.

38. Lord Jesus; transfuse me with your blood, in the name of Jesus.

39. Blood of Jesus; purge me from satanic deposit, in the name of Jesus.

40. Jehovah Rapha, heal me from any infirmity, in the name of Jesus.

41. Any evil pronouncement arising from infirmity; O Lord, destroy it with your fire, in the name of Jesus.

42. Let that power that raised Lazarus from the dead fall upon me now, in the name of Jesus.

43. Lord I thank you for your divine healing, in the name of Jesus.

PRAYERS TO BREAK YOKE OF HARDSHIP

1. Every arrow of hardship that is working powerfully against me, jump out and burn to ashes, in the name of Jesus.

2. Any power activating hardship in my life; be roasted by fire, in the name of Jesus.

3. Every altar crying hardship into my life; catch fire and burn to ashes, in the name of Jesus.

4. Any power prolonging hardship in my life; die suddenly by fire without any remedy, in the name of Jesus.

5. 1 claim instant deliverance from hardship by fire, in the name of Jesus.

6. Every yoke of hardship in my life; break by fire, in the name of Jesus.

7. Any power promoting hardship in my life; die, in the name of Jesus.

8. Any satanic arrow of unprofitable hard work fired against my life; backfire, in the name of Jesus.

9. Let all evil conspirators gathering against me be disbanded, in the name of Jesus.

10. Every deeply rooted problem in any area of my life; be uprooted and be roasted to ashes, in the name of Jesus.

11. Every yoke of foundational hardship; break by fire, in the name of Jesus.

12. Every garment of hardship covering my destiny; roast by fire, in the name of Jesus.

13. Every curse of hardship operating in my life; be melted by fire, in the name of Jesus.

14. Anointing of hardship, killing good things in my life; begin to kill yourself, in the name of Jesus.

15. I release myself from the bondage of hardship, in the name of Jesus.

16.   Every stubborn Goliath attacking me; die, in the name of Jesus.

17.   Lord, deliver me from this crocked generation, in the name of Jesus.

18.   Lord, deliver me from the camp of my enemy, in the name of Jesus.

19.   Every padlock of the enemy holding my breakthrough; break by fire, in the name of Jesus.

20.   Holy Spirit, before next week, I need a testimony, in the name of Jesus.

21.   I refuse to be associated with hardship, in the name of Jesus.

22.   I reject hardship in every area of my life, in the name of Jesus.

23.   Bondage of hardship; break, in the name of Jesus.

24.   Arrows of hardship; backfire, in the name of Jesus.

25. Any anointing of laboring in vain upon my life; dry up by fire, in the name of Jesus.

26. Any power, spirit and evil personality that have stolen my easy flow in life; release it and die, in the name of Jesus.

27. Power to dismantle hardship upon my life; possess me now, in the name of Jesus.

28. Foundational hardship in my family; die, in the name of Jesus.

29. Any mark of hardship in my life; be wiped off by the blood of Jesus, in the name of Jesus.

30. Any evil verdict issued against me to suffer in life; be revoked, in the name of Jesus.

31. Every twin brother/sister drinking the milk of my life; vomit it and die, in the name of Jesus.

32. Anointing of ease; fall upon me, in the name of Jesus.

33. Thank you, Lord, in the name of Jesus.

PRAYERS TO BREAK YOKE OF ALMOST THERE

1. Every spirit of almost there; what are you waiting for? Your time is up; die, in the name of Jesus.

2. Any power waging war against me at the edge of my breakthroughs; roast by fire, in the name of Jesus.

3. Every satanic warfare at the edge of my miracle; scatter by fire, in the name of Jesus.

4. Any power playing games with my miracles and breakthrough; die, in the name of Jesus.

5. Every satanic opposition to my breakthrough; scatter, in the name of Jesus.

6. Every altar of failure at the edge of my miracle; be demolished by fire, in the name of Jesus.

7. Every curse of failure at the edge of breakthrough operating my life; break, in the name of Jesus.

8. Let spirit of almost there that is working in my life perish, in the name of Jesus.

9. You oppressive spirits doing havoc in my life; come out with all your roots, in the name of Jesus.

10. I come against any power in heaven, on earth and underneath the earth that is against my wealth by the blood of Jesus, in the name of Jesus.

11. Let all those despising me begin to bow to me from now on, in the name of Jesus.

12. You spirit of Pisgah working against my progress; die, in the name of Jesus.

13. Every wicked yoke of almost there; break and release me, in the name of Jesus.

14. Any power of almost there, ready to disgrace me at the edge of my breakthrough; perish, in the name of Jesus.

15. I refuse to climb the mountain of almost there, in the name of Jesus.

16. I shall reach my goal and make it in life, in the name of Jesus.

17. Lord Jesus, push me into my breakthrough, in the name of Jesus.

18. The yoke of almost there in my life; break by fire, in the name of Jesus.

19. I reject every spirit of the tail in any areas of my life, in the name of Jesus.

20. Every dream of failure; disappear, in the name of Jesus.

21. Every curse of failure at the edge of breakthrough upon my life; break, in the name of Jesus.

22. Lord, let wonderful changes begin to be my lot from now, in the name of Jesus.

23. Anything that should die for me to be there and not almost there; die, in the name of Jesus.

24. Lord, remove covetousness from my eyes, in the name of Jesus.

25. Lord, turn me into untouchable coal of fire, in the name of Jesus.

26. Every evil spirit masquerading as friends; be exposed and disgraced, in the name of Jesus.

27. Every strongman pulling my life down; die, in the name of Jesus.

28. Any witchcraft power assigned against my life; wherever you are, die, in the name of Jesus.

29. Every evil mark placed on my destiny; be erased by the blood of Jesus, in Jesus' name.

30. Any demon that goes ahead of me to destroy my blessings; be destroyed by fire, in the name of Jesus.

31. I remove my name from the list of those seeing good things coming but never enjoy them, in the name of Jesus.

32. Any power painting me black in the mind of my helpers; die, in the name of Jesus.

33. Any curse placed on me that I will see or feel good things but I will not have it; break by fire, in the name of Jesus.

34. Lord, put my name in the list of those who see good things coming and enjoy it, in the name of Jesus.

35. I thank you Lord for answered prayers, in the name of Jesus.

PRAYERS TO BREAK YOKE OF CURSES

1.   Let all iron-like curses in my life be cut into pieces by the axe of God, in the name of Jesus.

2.   All self-imposed curse upon my life; receive total destruction by fire, in the name of Jesus.

3.   Any generational curse walking against me; scatter by fire, in the name of Jesus.

4.   Every parental curse flowing into my life; be terminated by fire, in the name of Jesus.

5.   Every curse coming from my refusal to pay tithes; be broken by the blood of Jesus, in Jesus' name.

6.   Let any curse arresting my family line be broken by the blood of Jesus, in Jesus' name.

7.   Holy Spirit, send your divine salt into my roots and purge it from every stubborn curse, in the name of Jesus.

8.   I release myself from any curse emanating from my past involvement with false religion, in the name of Jesus.

9.   I break and cancel any clinical and medical curse upon my life, in the name of Jesus.

10. I take authority over every curse of physical and spiritual destruction, in the name of Jesus.

11. Every curse of loneliness controlling my life; break, in the name of Jesus.

12. Every curse that is operating in my life as a result of the deeds of my ancestors, break and release me, in the name of Jesus.

13. Any curse issued by my parents, now operating in my life; break by fire, in the name of Jesus.

14. Any curse of untimely death operating in my family; break over my life, in the name of Jesus.

15. Any curse by my former boyfriend/girlfriend, affecting my marriage; break and release me, in the name of Jesus.

16. Any curse and limitations from my former masters/boss, expire, in the name of Jesus.

17. Lord, convert curses into blessings in my life, in the name of Jesus.

18. All multiple curses in my life; be broken, in the name of Jesus.

19. Every dream of failure in my life; disappear, in the name of Jesus.

20. Every curse of failure at the edge of success upon my life; break, in the name of Jesus.

21. Every yoke of almost there; break, in the name of Jesus.

22. Lord Jesus, let wonderful changes begin to be my lot from now on, in the name of Jesus.

23. Lord, deliver me from known and unknown curses, in the name of Jesus.

24. Holy Ghost fire, incubate my body, soul and spirit, in the name of Jesus.

25. All strongholds of curses in my life; be dashed to pieces, in the name of Jesus.

26. Every tongue that has rained incantations on me; roast by fire, in the name of Jesus.

27. Every bewitchment upon my life; be destroyed by fire, in the name of Jesus.

28. I break down the stronghold of witchcraft in my family, in the name of Jesus.

29. Let the counsel of the devil to destroy me be frustrated, in the name of Jesus.

30. Every evil yoke of curses upon my life; break and release me, in the name of Jesus.

31. Any evil decree that has been released against my life; backfire, in the name of Jesus.

32. Any inherited curses from my ancestors; be destroyed, in the name of Jesus.

33. Any curse in my parent's house that is destroying my destiny; receive destruction, in the name of Jesus.

34. Any curse of failure upon my life; break by fire, in the name of Jesus.

35. Any generational curses upon my life; break by fire, in the name of Jesus.

36. I receive arrow-proof and bulletproof jacket to disgrace curses, in the name of Jesus.

37. Lord, discharge your arrows against any curse disturbing my life, in the name of Jesus.

38. Every curse placed upon my life to divert my star; fall down and die, in the name of Jesus.

39. Curse of death in my life; die, in the name of Jesus.

40. Curse of poverty assigned against me; break, in the name of Jesus.

41. Curse of slavery holding me down; break by fire, in the name of Jesus.

42. Curse of problems in any area of my life; die, in the name of Jesus.

43. Lord Jesus, give me power against curses, in the name of Jesus.

44. Every satanic weapon, hidden yoke of curses in my life; break and release me, in the name of Jesus.

45. Stubborn powers behind every yoke of curses hanging over my life; receive judgment, in the name of Jesus.

46. Anointing to break every yoke of curse in my life; fall upon me, in the name of Jesus.

47. Iron yoke curses, manifesting in my family; be destroyed by the consuming fire of God, in the name of Jesus.

48. Every wicked personality, supervising evil yokes of curses in my life; die, in the name of Jesus.

49. Thank you, Lord, for prayer answered, in the name of Jesus.

PRAYERS TO BREAK YOKE OF REJECTION

1. Every label of rejection placed upon my life; I remove you and replace you with the label of favor and acceptance, in the name of Jesus.

2. You the strongman of rejection attached to my foundation; I shake you off into fire, in the name of Jesus.

3. Every stronghold of rejection, holding me into bondage; be dismantled and scatter by fire, in the name of Jesus.

4. You the mark of rejection placed upon my life, I wash you off by the blood of Jesus, in the name of Jesus.

5. Every garment of rejection designed for me; I cast you into the fire of judgment, in the name of Jesus.

6. Every cause or reason for rejection in my life; be destroyed completely by the blood of Jesus, in the name of Jesus.

7. Let men and women everywhere begin to show me favor and acceptance, in the name of Jesus.

8. Every yoke of rejection in my life and upon my life; break, in the name of Jesus.

9. Every seed of rejection planted in my life; be uprooted by fire, in the name of Jesus.

10. Though men may reject me; the Lord will never reject me, in the name of Jesus.

11. I rebuke every spirit of rejection in my life, in the name of Jesus.

12. Any power manipulating my life for evil; die, in the name of Jesus.

13. I shall not suffer rejection, in the name of Jesus.

14. Spirit of rejection in my life; die, in the name of Jesus.

15. Instead of rejection, I shall be favored, in the name of Jesus.

16. Powers promoting rejection in my life; die, in the name of Jesus.

17. I come against you with sword of fire, in the name of Jesus.

18. I banish you yoke of rejection from my life, in the name of Jesus.

19. Every mark of rejection in my body; be erased by the blood of Jesus, in the name of Jesus.

20. I refuse to be rejected from today, in the name of Jesus.

21. Every arrow of rejection; locate your sender, in the name of Jesus.

22. Every curse of rejection; locate me by fire, in the name of Jesus.

23. Every curse of rejection upon my life; break by fire, in the name of Jesus.

24. Any spirit of rejection that has possessed me; come out and die, in the name of Jesus.

25. Any pit of rejection that my inner man is occupying; I command you to jump out by fire, in the name of Jesus.

26. I am a child of God and I confess that the Spirit of God is in me; therefore, the yoke of rejection shall not prosper in my life, in the name of Jesus.

27. I reject and revoke the power behind rejection, in the name of Jesus.

28. I nullify and erase every mark of rejection by the blood of Jesus, in the name of Jesus.

29. I erase from my body the mark of rejection by the blood of Jesus, in the name of Jesus.

30. That evil yoke attached to rejection in my life; I break you by fire, by force, in the name of Jesus.

31. Goodness and mercy shall follow me all the days of my life, in the name of Jesus.

32. Spirit of rejection; I reject you, in the name of Jesus.

33. Any witchcraft veil on my face, roast by fire, in the name of Jesus.

34. Any evil hand that painted me with mud in my dream; wither, in the name of Jesus.

35. Any witchcraft urine on my body; be washed off by the blood of Jesus, in the name of Jesus.

36. Where I have been rejected in the past, I shall be accepted, in the name of Jesus.

37. Holy Spirit, spray your perfume of holiness on me, in the name of Jesus.

38. Thank you, Father for answered prayers, in the name of Jesus.

PRAYERS TO BREAK YOKE OF LIMITATION

1.   Every satanic limitation placed upon my life; break and release me, in the name of Jesus.

2.   The powers that are aborting my abilities in life; die, in the name of Jesus.

3.   All potential killers, assigned against my life; I choke you to death by the blood of Jesus and with the fire of God, in the name of Jesus.

4.   Every cage of the devil, stopping me from moving more than I am doing now; break and release my life by fire, in the name of Jesus.

5.   Let witchcraft embargo that is upon my life break and release me by fire, in the name of Jesus.

6.   Anointing to move forward by fire; fall upon my life now, in the name of Jesus.

7.   Any power struggling hard to limit my life; die, in the name of Jesus.

8.   Every yoke of limitation, placed upon my life; be lifted by fire, in the name of Jesus.

9.   Any power planning to turn my life upside down; fall down and die, in the name of Jesus.

10. I barricade my life from every satanic opinion, in the name of Jesus.

11. Let my divinely appointed helpers locate me from now, in the name of Jesus.

12. I break and renounce all evil soul ties I have had with anyone, in the name of Jesus.

13. Lord, cleanse me in body, soul, and spirit, in the name of Jesus.

14. I refuse to harbor any strange property in any department of my body, in the name of Jesus.

15. I release myself from any unconscious bondage, in the name of Jesus.

16. Spirit of limitation working in my life; your time is up; pack your load and get out, in the name of Jesus.

17. Blood of Jesus; it is my time to move from minimum to maximum, in the name of Jesus.

18. Spiritual basket working against my finances; catch fire and burn to ashes, in the name of Jesus.

19. I bind every desert spirit working against me, in the name of Jesus.

20. Every satanic stronghold erected against my progress; be pulled down, in the name of Jesus.

21. Lord Jesus, deliver me from the valley to the mountaintop, in the name of Jesus.

22. Lord Jesus, reveal myself to me, in the name of Jesus.

23. Any power pulling me down; die, in the name of Jesus.

24. I refuse to be caged by household enemies, in the name of Jesus.

25. I cancel every curse of limitation upon my life, in the name of Jesus.

26. Lord, enlarge my coast beyond my imaginations, in the name of Jesus.

27. Thou resurrection power of God; raise me from the dunghill, in the name of Jesus.

28. Any power of limitation on my life; die, in the name of Jesus.

29. Any yoke of limitation upon my life; break by fire, in the name of Jesus.

30. Any spirit of limitation that is manifesting in my life; die, in the name of Jesus.

31. Any evil personality that is limiting my potentials; die, in the name of Jesus.

32. I refuse to be limited, in the name of Jesus.

33. Any power, spirit and personality limiting my life; scatter by fire, in the name of Jesus.

34. My Father; place me where you want me to be, in the name of Jesus.

35. I shall not suffer limitation, in the name of Jesus.

36. Thank you, Lord, in the name of Jesus.

PRAYERS TO BREAK YOKE OF LONELINESS

1.	Any spirit of loneliness and rejection operating in my life; die, in the name of Jesus.

2.	Every curse of rejection in my foundation; break now, in the name of Jesus.

3.	Lord, my Comforter; comfort me, in the name of Jesus.

4.	Even though men have rejected me; the Lord will not reject me, in the name of Jesus.

5.	I will not be cast away, in the name of Jesus.

6.	You the strongman of loneliness attached to my life, die, in the name of Jesus.

7.	Every satanic altar of loneliness, working against my life; break, scatter and release my life by fire, in the name of Jesus.

8.	Every arrow of loneliness fired into my life; jump out and go back to sender, in the name of Jesus.

9.	The evil spirit that does not want me to marry; die suddenly, in the name of Jesus.

10.	Holy Spirit, raise good people who will keep me company, in the name of Jesus.

11. Any power keeping me in loneliness; die, in the name of Jesus.

12. Lord, break the yoke of loneliness in my life, in the name of Jesus.

13. Lord, separate me from loneliness, in the name of Jesus.

14. I shall not suffer loneliness, in the name of Jesus.

15. I refuse to be a friend to loneliness, in the name of Jesus.

16. Spirit of loneliness, reigning in my life; disappear, in the name of Jesus.

17. Loneliness; you will not wreck my life, in the name of Jesus.

18. By fire by force; loneliness, there is no hiding place for you in my life, in the name of Jesus.

19. Anything destroying my happiness, I command you to begin to destroy yourself, in the name of Jesus.

20. Any arrow of loneliness released into my life; backfire, in the name of Jesus.

21. Anointing to recover from loneliness; possess me now, in the name of Jesus.

22. Holy Ghost fire, circulate all over my body soul and spirit, in the name of Jesus.

23. I deliver myself from stagnancy, in the name of Jesus.

24. I refuse to be caged, in the name of Jesus.

25. I am not alone; the Comforter is with me, in the name of Jesus.

26. Every yoke of stagnancy in my life; break, in the name of Jesus.

27. I move forward by fire by force, in the name of Jesus.

28. Thou power of God; raise me from the pit of sorrow, in the name of Jesus.

29. I stand against any defeat in my dream, in the name of Jesus.

30. All my problems shall be converted to promotion, in me name of Jesus.

31. I refuse to die in loneliness, in the name of Jesus.

32. Any spirit that wants me to live a lonely life; die, in the name of Jesus

33. Every yoke of loneliness in my life; break, in the name of Jesus.

34. Every inherited curse of loneliness; break by fire, in the name of Jesus.

35. Every spirit of depression in my life; disappear by fire, in the name of Jesus.

36. Every inherited spirit of self-centeredness in my life; die, in the name of Jesus.

37. I shake off every shackles of loneliness in my life, in the name of Jesus.

38. Lord, connect me with good friends that will elevate my life, in the name of Jesus.

39. Thank you, God for giving me victory, in the name of Jesus.

PRAYERS TO BREAK YOKE OF WEAKNESS

1. I command every organ in my body to receive the fire of the Holy Ghost and the blood of Jesus, in the name of Jesus.

2. Let my God arise and put to flight every mind-controlling spirit, in the name of Jesus.

3. I reject every garment of confusion in my life, in the name of Jesus.

4. Let the anointing of spiritual knowledge fall upon me, in the name of Jesus.

5. The devil will not replace me in my service for the Lord, in the name of Jesus.

6. Spirit of weakness, go; divine strength come, in the name of Jesus.

7. Every arrow of weakness in my life from marine world; backfire, in the name of Jesus.

8. Lord Jesus, fill me afresh with your fire, in the name of Jesus.

9. Blood of Jesus, strengthen me, in the name of Jesus.

10. I shall not die with my weakness, in the name of Jesus.

11. Lord, wash me with your blood and deliver me, in the name of Jesus.

12. I come out of my slumber by fire, in the name of Jesus.

13. Lord, reckon me with the power of your might, in the name of Jesus.

14. I am strong in the Lord because the Lord has strengthened my weakness, in the name of Jesus.

15. I shall grow from strength to strength, in the name of Jesus.

16. I break every yoke of weakness by fire, in the name of Jesus.

17. Any seed of weakness in my life; catch fire and burn to ashes, in the name of Jesus.

18. Any arrow of weakness that has been released into my life; backfire, in the name of Jesus.

19. Any yoke of weakness in my life; break, in the name of Jesus.

20. You spirit of weakness; I bury you today, in the name of Jesus.

21. You spirit of weakness; I replace you today with the strength of God, in the name of Jesus.

22. Any power causing weakness in my life; die, in the name of Jesus.

23. Power over weakness; fall upon me, in the name of Jesus.

24. I shall not suffer weakness, in the name of Jesus.

25. Every arrow of weakness fired into my life; backfire, in name of Jesus.

26. Every spirit of weakness controlling my life; die, in the name of Jesus.

27. Every physical and spiritual weakness in my life; disappear now, in the name of Jesus.

28. Let my weakness become strength, in the name of Jesus.

29. Let every dead organ in my life receive life, in the name of Jesus.

30. Every spirit of weakness controlling my life; die, in the name of Jesus.

31. Thank you, Lord for strengthening me, in the name of Jesus.

PRAYERS TO BREAK YOKE OF SATAN

1.   Every satanic spreading river in my life; dry up, in the name of Jesus.

2.   Every satanic deposit in my life; be flushed out by the blood of Jesus, in the name of Jesus.

3.   You that power controlling my destiny; my life is not your candidate, in the name of Jesus.

4.   Every satanic inspired sickness in my life; disappear, in the name of Jesus.

5.   I reject every property of Satan prepared for me, in the name of Jesus.

6.   Plantation of Satan; die in my life, in the name of Jesus.

7.   Materials of Satan in my life; catch fire, in the name of Jesus.

8.   Lord Jesus, deliver me from every satanic power, in the name of Jesus.

9.   Anything in my life co-operating with Satan, die; in the name of Jesus.

10.   I come out from the yoke of Satan, in the name of Jesus.

11.   Satan; I speak total destruction unto you today, in the name of Jesus.

12.   Yoke of Satan in any area of my life; bum to ashes, in the name of Jesus.

13.   Satan; lose your hold over my life, in the name of Jesus.

14.   My money with the strongman of Satan; be released, in the name of Jesus.

15.   I forbid Satan to kill me for any reason, in the name of Jesus.

16.   Satan; you are a liar; you cannot bring me down, in the name of Jesus.

17.   Any satanic embargo upon my life; receive destruction, in the name of Jesus.

18.   Any satanic plan to terminate my life; scatter, by fire, in the name of Jesus.

19.   By the anointing of God; I reject satanic suggestions and report for my life, in the name of Jesus.

20.	Satanic visitors in my life; die, in the name of Jesus.

21.	Greater is He that is in me than he that is in the world, in the name of Jesus.

22.	I am a child of God; Satan; get thee behind me, in the name of Jesus.

23.	Any satanic influence upon my life; I cast you into the lake of fire, in the name of Jesus.

24.	Thou power that raised Jesus from the dead; deliver me from satanic stronghold, in the name of Jesus.

25.	My Lord Jesus has given me more life and His salvation is round about me greatly, in the name of Jesus.

26.	Every yoke of satanic manipulation; break, in the name of Jesus.

27.	I refuse and rebuke every strategy of Satan, in the name of Jesus.

28.	My Lord and my God; raise intercessors to stand in the gap for me always, in the name of Jesus.

29.	Father Lord, show me an immeasurable forgiveness daily in my life, in the name of Jesus.

30. Any demonically organized seductive appearance to pull me down; be rendered null and void, in the name of Jesus.

31. Let every demonic trap, set against my life be shattered to pieces, in the name of Jesus.

32. I reject all uncontrollable crying, heaviness and regrets, in the name of Jesus.

33. Thank you, Father for saving me, in the name of Jesus.

PRAYERS TO BREAK YOKE OF EVIL PATTERN

1. I release myself from inherited bondage, in the name of Jesus.

2. I break and loose myself from every inherited curse, in the name of Jesus.

3. I break all the curses of deformity, infirmity and sickness in both sides of my family, back to the tenth generations, in the name of Jesus.

4. Every spirit of death, struggling to take my life; fail woefully, in the name of Jesus.

5. I refuse to inherit the evil pattern of my ancestors, in the name of Jesus.

6. Every garment of evil pattern in my family line, burn to ashes, in the name of Jesus.

7. Every pattern of non-achievement in my family line; clear out, in the name of Jesus.

8. You evil pattern of poverty in my family line; I blot you out by the blood of Jesus, in the name of Jesus.

9. Every witchcraft river, flowing against my life; dry up to your roots, in the name of Jesus.

10. Holy Spirit divine, take absolute control of my life, in the name of Jesus.

11. Every evil counsel of Satan; be nullified by the blood of Jesus, in the name of Jesus.

12. I release myself from any evil pattern of the enemy, in the name of Jesus.

13. Lord, restore me from any evil way that the enemy has put me into, in the name of Jesus.

14. Every yoke of evil pattern; break by fire, in the name of Jesus.

15. Lord, open my eyes to see You, in the name of Jesus.

16. Any evil way of life in me; die, in the name of Jesus.

17. Any altar of evil pattern in my life; catch fire, in the name of Jesus.

18. Any horn of evil pattern that has been rising in my life; die, in the name of Jesus.

19. Anointing to live a godly life; possess me now, in the name of Jesus.

20. Every curse hanging on my family tree; be broken, in the name of Jesus.

21. Every curse with long legs in my family; break, in the name of Jesus.

22. I release myself from any inherited bondage, in the name of Jesus.

23. I break and loose myself from every collective curse, in the name of Jesus.

24. I break and loose myself from every collective evil covenant, in the name of Jesus.

25. Evil pattern, die compulsorily forever in my life, in the name of Jesus.

26. I refuse to accept evil pattern in my life, in the name of Jesus.

27. I destroy the yoke of evil pattern operating in every area of my life, in the name of Jesus.

28. Evil pattern of slavery in my life; die in the name of Jesus.

29. Evil pattern of failure in my life; die, in the name of Jesus.

30. I claim power over evil pattern assigned against me, in the name of Jesus.

31. I thank you Lord for delivering me from evil pattern, in the name of Jesus.

PRAYERS TO BREAK YOKE OF BACK TO SQUARE ONE

1. All ye strongmen in my life; hear ye the word of the Living God; my life is going to move forward by fire, in the name of Jesus.

2. Any power that is working to set my life backwards, die by fire, in the name of Jesus.

3. Any spirit of backwardness, caging my life; release me and die, in the name of Jesus.

4. Every arrow of setback, fired into my life; go back to sender, in the name of Jesus.

5. Any spirit of disappointment, operating in my life; perish by fire, in the name of Jesus.

6. Power of non-achievement in my life; die, in the name of Jesus.

7. Let powers of emptier die in my life, in the name of Jesus.

8. Lord Jesus, move me forward forever, in the name of Jesus.

9. Arrows of back to square one; backfire, in the name of Jesus.

10. Yoke of back to square one upon my life; break, in the name of Jesus.

11. You my enemies; I refuse to go back to square one, in the name of Jesus.

12. Instead of going back to square one; I shall move forward by fire, in the name of Jesus.

13. My enemy; my problem is over; it is now your turn, therefore, carry your load, in the name of Jesus.

14. I claim uncommon success in my daily activity, in the name of Jesus.

15. Anointing to disgrace my problems; fall on me, in the name of Jesus.

16. Lord Jesus, let not your investment in my life be wasted, in the name of Jesus.

17. Any evil hand that is pulling me backwards in life; receive fire, in the name of Jesus.

18. Any power that is destroying my life; die, in the name of Jesus.

19. Any covenant relationship between backwardness and me; break by fire, in the name of Jesus.

20. The power to move forward; possess me now, in the name of Jesus.

21. Lord Jesus, deliver me from the spirit of the valley, in the name of Jesus.

22. I shall not go back to my vomit, in the name of Jesus.

23. I drink the blood of Jesus to strengthen my position in the Lord, in the name of Jesus.

24. The Rock of Ages is my strength; therefore, I refuse to go back to square one, in the name of Jesus.

25. No retreat, no surrender. My Lord Jesus is my Redeemer; and I stand on His word, in the name of Jesus.

26. I refuse to turn back to Sodom and Gomorrah, and Egypt, in the name of Jesus.

27. Every cycle of repeated problems in my life; break, in the name of Jesus.

28. Any power that afflicted my parents and is now pursuing me; die, in the name of Jesus.

29. I refuse every left-over hardship of my parents, in the name of Jesus.

30.   Every spirit of backwardness, working against my destiny; die, in the name of Jesus.

31.   My life; move forward by fire, in the name of Jesus.

32.   Thank you, God for Your salvation, in the name of Jesus.

PRAYERS TO BREAK YOKE OF FEAR

1.   Every torment of fear upon my life; perish, in the name of Jesus.

2.   Even though I walk through the valley of the shadow of death, I will not fear, in the name of Jesus.

3.   Any power of failure afflicting me with the spirit of fear; fail now, in the name of Jesus.

4.   Any power of fear hindering me from moving forward; die, in the name of Jesus.

5.   Thou bondage of fear in my foundation; break, in the name of Jesus.

6.   Sting of fear and failure; release my mind, in the name of Jesus.

7. Sting of death; release my mind, in the name of Jesus.

8. I command satanic table upon which he exhibits his evil in my heart to receive the fire of God, in the name of Jesus.

9. Arrow of fear fired against my life; backfire by fire, in the name of Jesus.

10. Blood of Jesus; replenish my heart, in the name of Jesus.

11. Lord, you are my Light and Salvation, so I will not fear, in the name of Jesus.

12. I refuse to fear in my life, in the name of Jesus.

13. My tomorrow is blessed in Christ. Therefore, you spirit of fear; die, in the name of Jesus.

14. Every yoke of fear upon my life; die, in the name of Jesus.

15. The spirit of power, love and sound mind is my weapon. Therefore, fear; go out, in the name of Jesus!

16. I break the covenant attached to the spirit of fear in my life, in the name of Jesus.

17. I refuse to be in bondage of fear, in the name of Jesus.

18. Demonic nightmare is not my lot. Therefore, fear; die, in the name of Jesus.

19. Any evil power intimidating my life; die, in the name of Jesus.

20. You fear that wants to destroy my life; come out and die, in the name of Jesus.

21. You spirit that wants to swallow my life by the power of God; swallow yourself and die, in the name of Jesus.

22. Anointing to withstand fear; possess me now, in name of Jesus.

23. I bind and cast out every spirit of fear in my life, in the name of Jesus.

24. I break and loose myself from every grip of fear, in the name of Jesus.

25. By the power in the blood of Jesus, I overcome the spirit of fear, in the name of Jesus.

26. From today, I overcome you spirit of fear, in the name of Jesus.

27. Holy Ghost fire; consume the spirit of fear, in the name of Jesus.

28. Lord Jesus, banish this spirit of fear from me forever, in the name of Jesus.

29. I receive power over fear, in the name of Jesus.

30. Lord Jesus, deliver me from the spirit of fear, in the name of Jesus.

31. Power of boldness; fall upon my life, in the name of' Jesus.

32. Inherited spirit of fear; wherever you are, die, in the name of Jesus.

33. I jump out from the captivity of fear, in the name of Jesus.

34. Thank you, Lord, in the name of Jesus.

PRAYERS TO BREAK YOKE OF SPIRITUAL MARRIAGE

1. By the power in the blood of Jesus; I release myself from the bondage of evil spiritual marriage, in the name of Jesus.

2. I denounce every evil spiritual marriage, in the name of Jesus.

3. Every spirit of lateness in marriage, operating in my life; die, in the name of Jesus.

4. I break every covenant with the spirit husband/ wife, in the name of Jesus.

5. Every evil soul-tie hindering my marriage; break, in the name of Jesus.

6. Ancestral spiritual marriage covenant; die, in the name of Jesus

7. Stubborn yoke of spiritual marriage, die, in the name of Jesus.

8. Powers in charge of spiritual marriage in my life; die, in the name of Jesus.

9. I claim deliverance from spiritual marriage, in the name of Jesus.

10. Spiritual marriage in my life; die, in the name of Jesus.

11. Yoke of spiritual marriage; break instantly, in the name of Jesus.

12. Evil spiritual marriage; I receive the power of God to disgrace you, in the name of Jesus.

13. I speak death unto spiritual marriage; and you shall rise no more, in the name of Jesus.

14. My life is not available for you; so, locate your sender, in the name of Jesus.

15. Spirit husband/wife; release me by fire, in the name of Jesus.

16. Every foundation of spirit husband/wife in my family line; be dismantled, in the name of Jesus.

17. I break every marriage covenant with spirit husband/wife by the blood of Jesus, in the name of Jesus.

18. I break every marriage vow with spirit husband/wife, in the name of Jesus.

19. Holy Ghost fire; break and loose me from the hold of spirit husband/wife, in the name of Jesus.

20. You the strongman that has wedded me in the realms of the spirit; receive fire and die, in the name of Jesus.

21. You the strongman that has covenanted me through spiritual marriage; by the power of God, die, in the name of Jesus.

22. I renounce any spiritual marriage working against my life, in the name of Jesus.

23. Lord Jesus, deliver me from the bondage of spiritual marriage, in the name of Jesus.

24. Any decision taken in the waters against me; be cancelled, in the name of Jesus.

25. Marine witchcraft planning evil spiritual marriage for me; die, in the name of Jesus.

26. Any marine boy or girl, whispering to me in my dream; be deaf and dumb by fire, in the name of Jesus.

27. Power of God; destroy every spiritual marriage in my life, in the name of Jesus.

28. You queen of heaven introducing useless spouse to me; I am not your candidate. Therefore, die with your children, in the name of Jesus.

29. I cover my dream life with the blood of Jesus; and barricade it with the fire of the Holy Ghost, in the name of Jesus.

30. Any marine witchcraft, posing as my husband/wife in my dream; die, in the name of Jesus.

31. Any evil personality alive or dead that has taken my dowry in the realm of the spirit; perish with your money, in the name of Jesus.

32. Any marine witch posing as my child in my dream; die, in the name of Jesus.

33. Any evil materials exchanged between me and the spirit husband/wife in my life; catch fire and burn to ashes, in the name of Jesus;

34. You spirit husband/wife in my life; I divorce you now, in the name of Jesus.

35. Thank you, Father, in the name of Jesus.

PRAYERS TO BREAK YOKE OF PLACENTA BONDAGE

1. I break and release myself from the evil effect of placenta bondage, in the name of Jesus.

2. Every satanic manipulation of my destiny; be nullified, in the name of Jesus.

3. I break and loose myself from the spirit of non-achievement, in the name of Jesus.

4. Any form of parental curse placed on me consciously or unconsciously; break by fire, in the name of Jesus.

5. Every garment of shame and reproach; catch fire now and burn to ashes, in the name of Jesus.

6. Eaters of flesh and drinkers of blood; vomit my placenta, in the name of Jesus.

7. Every witchcraft coven and marine base; release my placenta, in the name of Jesus.

8. Every covenant between my placenta and the grave; be broken, in the name of Jesus.

9. Every power utilizing my placenta to summon by spirit; I break your power, in the name of Jesus.

10. If my placenta has been used to divert my destiny, O God, arise; and change it now, in the name of Jesus.

11. Lord Jesus, deliver me from inherited bondage, in the name of Jesus.

12. Any power from my father's house controlling my destiny; die, in the name of Jesus.

13. Any Power from my mother's house remote-controlling my destiny; be crushed against the Rock of Ages, in the name of J Jesus.

14. Any satanic power, keeping my placenta for evil; O God of vengeance; fight for me, in the name of Jesus.

15. Any witchcraft coven manipulating my placenta; wherever you are; die, in the name of Jesus.

16. Any marine witchcraft holding my placenta in the water; let your water be dried up and be consumed by fire, in the name of Jesus.

17. I break every curse issued against me as a result of the generational curse, in the name of Jesus.

18. Thou yoke of our Lord Jesus' anointing; break all evil yoke in my life, in the name of Jesus.

19. By fire by force, I recover my placenta from witchcraft control, in the name of Jesus.

20. Any placenta bondage in my life; die, in the name of Jesus.

21. I release myself from placenta bondage, in the name of Jesus.

22. Any power using my placenta against my life; die, in the name of Jesus.

23. Any yoke of placenta bondage in my life; break by fire, in the name of Jesus.

24. Lord Jesus, deliver me from placenta bondage, in the name of Jesus.

25. Every power using my placenta against me; die, in the name of Jesus.

26. Every covenant between me and placenta bondage; break, in the name of Jesus.

27. Any power in the water; release my placenta, in the name of Jesus.

28. Every cage of placenta manipulation; break, in the name of Jesus.

29.   My placenta; hear the word of the Living God: refuse to cooperate with my enemies, in the name of Jesus!

30.   You my placenta; receive deliverance, in the name of Jesus.

31.   Placenta bondage in my life; die, in the name of Jesus.

32.   By fire by force, I am free from placenta bondage, in the name of Jesus.

33.   I thank you Lord, in the name of Jesus.

PRAYERS TO BREAK YOKE OF WATER SPIRITS

1. I break and loose myself from the association of water spirits, in the name of Jesus.

2. Lord my God; speak destruction into the kingdom of the marine spirits, in the name of Jesus.

3. Every covenant, binding me with the marine kingdom; break and release me, in the name of Jesus.

4. I withdraw myself from the evil association of water spirits, in the name of Jesus.

5. By the power in the blood of Jesus, I break every evil spiritual marriage vow, in the name of Jesus.

6. Any power in the water ruling my life; come out, in the name of Jesus.

7. Any strange water in my life; come out, in the name of Jesus.

8. Any area of my life captured by water spirit; be released by thunder and fire of God, in the name of Jesus.

9. Thou yoke of water spirits; break forever, in the name of Jesus.

10. My Father; set me free, in the name of Jesus.

11. I pollute my water with the blood of Jesus, in the name of Jesus.

12. Lord Jesus, deliver me by your power, in the name of Jesus.

13. You water spirit yoke; break and lose your hold over my life, in the name of Jesus.

14. I break every dedication to water spirit, in the name of Jesus.

15. Every deposit of water spirit in my life; be flushed out by the blood of Jesus, in the name of Jesus.

16. Every trademark of water spirit; be shaken out of my life, in the name of Jesus.

17. Every area of cooperation with water spirit in my life; be broken, in the name of Jesus.

18. Any blood and water pollution of my body; come out, in the name of Jesus

19. You that water spirit working against my life; die, in the name of Jesus.

20. Any property of the water spirits in all departments of my life; receive fire and burn to ashes, in the name of Jesus.

21. You combined powers from the water, gathering against me; scatter by fire, in the name of Jesus.

22. Any agent on assignment from the waters against my destiny; I command you to die, in the name of Jesus.

23. Anointing to deal with powers from the waters; possess me now, in the name of Jesus.

24. Holy Ghost, clothe me with your garment of fire, in the name of Jesus

25. Any power of marine witchcraft holding my blessings in bondage; die, in the name of Jesus.

26. Any water spirit from my place of birth; die by fire, in the name of Jesus.

27. Every agent of marine witchcraft, physically attached to my destiny; wherever you are; die, in the name of Jesus.

28. Every evil altar in the water practicing witchcraft against me; roast by fire, in the name of Jesus.

29. Any evil mirror used by marine powers to monitor me; crash to irreparable pieces, in the name of Jesus.

30. Any evil yoke attached to the power in the water; break by fire, in the name of Jesus.

31. Every grip of water spirit upon my life; lose your hold, in the name of Jesus.

32. Every evil dedication of my life to water spirits; be destroyed, in the name of Jesus.

33. Any spirit from the waters demanding my worship; die, in the name of Jesus.

34. I divorce any marriage between me and water spirit, in the name of Jesus.

35. Lord, build your wall of fire around me to scare away any water spirit from reaching me, in the name of Jesus.

36. Thank you, Lord, in the name of Jesus.

PRAYERS TO BREAK YOKE OF
POWERLESSNESS

1. Every arrow of powerlessness fired into my life; backfire, in the name of Jesus.

2. Let every spiritual weakness turn into spiritual strength, in the name of Jesus.

3. Every anti-power bondage in my life; break by fire, in the name of Jesus.

4. Lord, wake me up from any form of spiritual slumber; and help me put on the armor of revival fire, in the name of Jesus.

5. Any power from my father's house, rendering me powerless; die, in the name of Jesus.

6. Arrow of sin fired at me to render me powerless; go back to your sender, in the name of Jesus.

7. All ashes on my prayer altar; be blown off, in the name of Jesus.

8. Lord, by your power; strengthen me, in the name of Jesus.

9. Lord, convert my weakness to Your divine power, in the name of Jesus.

10. Lord, quench not Your Holy Spirit in me, in the name of Jesus.

11. Lord, let my life be in You, in the name of Jesus.

12. Remember me O Lord, in the name of Jesus.

13. I stand against every spirit of prayerlessness; and I cast it into the lake of fire, in the name of Jesus.

14. The power of praying without ceasing; fall upon my life, in the name of Jesus.

15. Lord, deliver me from the spirit of slumber and move me forward by fire, in the name of Jesus.

16. Let the fire of God fall upon my prayer life, in the name of Jesus.

17. The anointing of powerlessness in my life; dry up by fire, in the name of Jesus.

18. Every coldness in my spiritual life; disappear, in the name of Jesus.

19. Any power that wants to swallow my prayer life; swallow fire and die, in the name of Jesus.

20. Any seed of weakness that exists in my life; become strength, in the name of Jesus.

21. You evil personality contending with my prayer life; die, in the name of Jesus.

22. Every attack against my prayer altar; backfire, in the name of Jesus.

23. Lord, strengthen my prayer altar with your fire, in the name of Jesus.

24. Every evil arrow fired against my prayer altar; go back to your sender, in the name of Jesus.

25. Lord, possess me completely, in the name of Jesus.

26. I release myself from the bondage of prayerlessness, in the name of Jesus.

27. I come out from the cage of prayerlessness, in the name of Jesus.

28. Any power seating on my prayer life; die, in the name of Jesus.

29. Fire of revival; fall upon my prayer life, in the name of Jesus.

30. Every yoke of prayerlessness; I neutralize you with the blood of Jesus, in the name of Jesus.

31. I reject you spirit of prayerlessness, in the name of Jesus.

32. Spirit of slumber; die, in the name of Jesus,

33. Thank you, Lord, for reviving my prayer life, in the name of Jesus.

PRAYERS TO BREAK YOKE OF SETBACK

1. Every curse of setback placed upon my life; break, in the name of Jesus

2. All evil spirits troubling my life; be bound, in the name of Jesus.

3. The pregnancy of good things within me shall not be aborted, in the name of Jesus.

4. All the seats of affairs in my life will not be in vain, in the name of Jesus.

5. Any cold, blocking the sunlight of my glory and breakthroughs; be dispersed, in the name of Jesus.

6. Yoke of setback, break by fire, in the name of Jesus.

7. Arrows of setback; backfire and locate your sender, in the name of Jesus.

8. Every setback arranged for my destiny; I disorganize you, in the name of Jesus.

9. Every plant of setback; scatter by fire, in the name of Jesus.

10. Setback spirit in my life; die, in the name of Jesus.

11. I claim deliverance from the spirit of setback, in the name of Jesus.

12. Any power causing backwardness in my life; die, in the name of Jesus.

13. By the blood of Jesus; I loose myself from this wicked spirit of setback, in the name of Jesus.

14. I break myself free from every curse of setback, in the name of Jesus.

15. You ground; carry judgment against every power working against me, in the name of Jesus.

16. Holy Ghost; liberate my life for signs and wonders, in the name of Jesus.

17. Lord Jesus, move me forward by fire in the name of Jesus.

18. Any power that is sending me back, die in shame, in the name of Jesus.

19. I refuse to give up, in the name of Jesus.

20. You that Goliath, resisting my forward movement in life; die, in the name of Jesus.

21. Any chain of setback upon my life, break by fire, in the name of Jesus.

22. Anointing to match forward; possess me now, in the name of Jesus.

23. I can do all things through Christ who strengthens me, in the name of Jesus.

24. Lord Jesus, reveal myself to me, in the name of Jesus.

25. Every dream attacker manipulating my life; die, in the name of Jesus.

26. I reject the counsel of the enemy by fire, in the name of Jesus.

27. Any remote-controlling power from my father's and mother's house; be dashed into irreparable pieces, in the name of Jesus.

28. Thou power of the Living God; fill my body, soul, and spirit with your word, in the name of Jesus.

29. I stand on the Rock of Ages; therefore, I shall not fall, in the name of Jesus.

30. Every cycle of backwardness in my life, break, in the name of Jesus.

31. Foundational bondage setting me back in life, break, in the name of Jesus,

32. Any mark of backwardness in my life, be wiped off, in the name of Jesus.

33. My eagle shall fly once again, in the name of Jesus.

34. Thank you, Father, for moving me forward, in the name of Jesus.

PRAYERS TO BREAK YOKE OF RECURRING PROBLEMS

1. Any repeated problem in my life, die, in the name of Jesus.

2. You that chronic infirmity in my life, die, in the name of Jesus.

3. Every curse of repeated problem upon my life, break by thunder, in the name of Jesus.

4. God, arise and let all the enemies of my progress scatter, in the name of Jesus.

5. All the keys to my goodness still in the possession of the enemy, O Lord, give them unto me, in the name of Jesus.

6. Affliction shall not rise the second time in my life, in the name of Jesus.

7. Any problem that has vowed to die with me, be buried now, in the name of Jesus.

8. Any ladder of darkness through which the enemy climbed into my life, be roasted by fire, in the name of Jesus.

9. Any problem programmed into the air against me, be blown back to the sender, in the name of Jesus.

10. Lord, convert my problem to promotion, in the name of Jesus.

11. Lord, deliver me from every evil inheritance from my father's house, in the name of Jesus.

12. God, answer me by the fire of Elijah, in the name of Jesus.

13. Holy Ghost fire, incubate my body soul and spirit with unquenchable fire, in the name of Jesus.

14. I am a child of God. Therefore, I fire back any evil curse to sender, in the name of Jesus.

15. Every evil yoke of repeated problem, break by fire, in the name of Jesus.

16. My problems shall be converted to promotions, in the name of Jesus.

17. Repeated problems in my life, backfire, in the name of Jesus.

18. Any power reviving problems in my life, die, in the name of Jesus.

19:     Any repeated problems that want to destroy my life, be destroyed by fire, in the name of Jesus.

20.   Anointing to destroy repeated problems, possess me now, in the name of Jesus.

21.   Any problem in my life inherited from my parents, die, in the name of Jesus.

22.   Any repeated problem, I bury you alive, in the name of Jesus.

23.   Every power sponsoring failure in my life, die, in the name of Jesus.

24.   I receive anointing to overcome repeated problems, in the name of Jesus.

25.   I release myself from bewitchment, in the name of Jesus.

26.   I release myself from mistakes, in the name of Jesus.

27.   Curse of manipulation; break, in the name of Jesus.

28.   Enchantment of errors, die, in the name of Jesus.

29.   Lord Jesus, empower me by fire, in the name of Jesus.

30. You repeated problems, I block your entry. I bury you forever, in the name of Jesus.

31. Thank you, Lord, in the name of Jesus.

PRAYERS TO BREAK YOKE OF UNFORGIVINGNESS

1. Every seed of unforgiveness planted in my life, be uprooted by fire, in the name of Jesus.

2. Any spirit of unforgiveness hindering my blessings, die, in the name of Jesus.

3. Lord my God, give me the grace to forgive those who offend me, in the name Jesus.

4. Every spirit of bitterness in my life, die, in the name of Jesus.

5. You spirit of bondage, Luke warmness and perdition, operating in my life, die, in the name of Jesus.

6. Unforgiveness, melt by the fire of the Almighty God, in the name of Jesus.

7. Spirit of unforgiveness, depart from me today, in the name of Jesus

8. I command the spirit of unforgiveness to die, in the name of Jesus.

9. Unforgiving power, I banish you out of my life, in the name of Jesus.

10. You spirit of hardness of the heart, die, in the name of Jesus.

11. You spirit of revenge, die, in the name of Jesus

12. You spirit of witchcraft, die, in the name of Jesus.

13. Lord, give me a new heart, in the name of Jesus.

14. Every yoke of unforgiveness, break, in the name of Jesus.

15. I command the spirit of unforgiveness to die, in the name of Jesus.

16. I release myself from the power of unforgiveness, in the name of Jesus.

17. You, evil powers that are beautifying unforgiving spirit in my life, die, in the name of Jesus.

18. Lord, break me down and rebuild me, in the name of Jesus,

19. You anger in my heart, receive coldness, in the name of Jesus.

20. By the power of God, I refuse to have an unforgiving heart, in the name of Jesus.

21. You that mountain of unforgiveness in my life, collapse and die, in the name of Jesus.

22. I issue this warning to you Satan, get behind me and leave me alone, in the name of Jesus!

23. I am a child of the Living God, therefore, unforgiveness is not my lot, in the name of Jesus.

24. Father Lord, break any stony unforgiving heart, in the name of Jesus.

25. Every evil inner voice of hatred, be silenced forever, in the name of Jesus.

26. I refuse to live in the past, in the name of Jesus.

27. Every evil advisor misleading me, be paralyzed, in the name of Jesus.

28. Any inherited spirit of unforgiveness in my family, die, in the name of Jesus.

PRAYERS TO BREAK EVIL APPETITE

1. I release myself from demonic pollution, emanating from the evil appetite in my life, in the name of Jesus.

2. Every ancestral demonic pollution in my life, release me and die, in the name of Jesus

3. I refuse to be addicted to unprofitable things, in the name of Jesus.

4. Evil appetite in my life; die, in the name of Jesus.

5. You spirit of evil appetite in my life, hear the Word of the Living God, if I live; I live for Jesus. Therefore, die, in the name of Jesus.

6. Every evil appetite for food in my life, die, in the name of Jesus.

7. Every evil appetite for sex in my life, die, in the name of Jesus.

8. Power of self-control, possess my life, in the name of Jesus.

9. Appetite for the Word of God and prayers, possess me now, in the name of Jesus.

10. Lord, perfect what is lacking in my life, in the name of Jesus.

11. Every general curse placed upon my life, die by fire, in the name of Jesus.

12. That power that draws me to sin, die by fire, in the name of Jesus.

13. I come against you the strongman of evil yoke of appetite, in the name of Jesus.

14. Holy Ghost fire, enter into my foundation by fire, in the name of Jesus.

15. Any power that makes me to eat too much, die, in the name of Jesus.

16. Any power using food to trap me down, die, in the name of Jesus.

17. Any arrow of evil appetite released into my life, backfire, in the name of Jesus.

18. My belly will not control me, I will control my belly and my appetite, in the name of Jesus.

19. Lord, deliver me from the power of sin, in the name of Jesus.

20. I command the power of sin in my life to die, in the name of Jesus.

21. Lord, crucify my flesh on your cross, in the name of Jesus.

22.   Every yoke of sin in my life, break, in the name of Jesus.

23.   Any form of bewitchment in my life, die, in the name of Jesus.

24.   Any form of manipulation in my life, die, in the name of Jesus.

25.   Sprits of bad habits, die, in the name of Jesus.

26.   Lord, break the yoke of evil appetite in my life, in the name of Jesus.

27.   Set me free O Lord by Your power, in the name of Jesus.

28.   I replace every evil appetite with godly appetite for the Word of God and prayer, in the name of Jesus.

29.   I refuse to allow evil appetite to destroy my life, in the name of Jesus.

30.   Every evil appetite opening way for sin in my life, roast by fire, in the name of Jesus.

31.   Thank You Father, in the name of Jesus.

PRAYERS TO BREAK YOKE OF IMPOSSIBILITY

1. Every plantation of impossibility in my life, be roasted, in the name of Jesus.

2. God of possibility, take control of every stubborn problem in my life, in the name of Jesus.

3. Impossibilities shall not be my portion, in the name of Jesus.

4. Every curse of impossibility in my foundation, break, in the name of Jesus.

5. Every yoke of impossibility, caging my life, break, in the name of Jesus.

6. Yokes of impossibility are becoming possible by fire, in the name of Jesus.

7. I claim victory now over impossibility, in the name of Jesus.

8. Every plan of impossibility against my life, scatter, in the name of Jesus.

9. Impossibility, hear me very well; my life is not available for you. Therefore, die, in the name of Jesus.

10. My impossibilities have become possible, in the name of Jesus.

11. You, root of impossibility in my life, be uprooted by fire, in the name of Jesus.

12. I receive power to overcome impossible situations, in the name of Jesus.

13. Let every mark of impossibility be rubbed off from every department of my life, in the name of Jesus.

14. My situation, change by fire, in the name of Jesus.

15. Curse of impossibility, jump out of my life, in the name of Jesus.

16. You impossibility, lose your position in my life, in the name of Jesus.

17. I destroy every demonic net working against me, in the name of Jesus.

18. I withdraw my name from the register of impossibility, in the name of Jesus.

19. Every mountain of impossibility in my life, receive deadly destruction, in the name of Jesus.

20. Any Goliath, making things so hard for my life, die, in the name of Jesus.

21. Lord, revive the David of my life to destroy the Goliath of my problems, in the name of Jesus.

22. You problems that want to make me useless, I command you to be destroyed, in the name of Jesus.

23. Power to overthrow the seat of my impossibility, possess me now, in the name of Jesus.

24. For with God all things are possible. Therefore, strongholds of impossibility are being uprooted, in the name of Jesus.

25. Power of the living God, make impossible situations in my life possible, in the name of Jesus.

26. Every yoke of impossibility, break by fire, in the name of Jesus.

27. God, arise and fight for me, in the name of Jesus.

28. Arrows of impossibility fired at me, back fire by fire, in name of Jesus.

29. Blood of Jesus, make it impossible for the enemy to track down my star from the realm of the spirit, in the name of Jesus.

30. Let witchcraft embargo on my way to progress be dismantled by fire, in the name of Jesus.

31. Lord, convert my problems to promotions, in the name of Jesus.

32. God, thank You for making all things possible for me, in the name of Jesus.

THANK YOU!

I'd like to use this time to thank you for purchasing my books and helping my ministry and work. Any copy of my book you buy helps to fund my ministry and family, as well as offering much-needed inspiration to keep writing. My family and I are very thankful, and we take your assistance very seriously.

You have already accomplished so much, but I would appreciate an honest review of some of my books through the link below. This is critical since reviews reflect how much an author's work is respected.

Please [click here] to leave a review on Amazon. If you're viewing from a printed version, please visit amazon.com/review/create-review?asin=1545144214 to leave a review.

Please be aware that I read and value all comments and reviews. You can always post a review even though you haven't finished the book yet, and then edit your reviews later.

Thank you so much as you spare a precious moment of your time and may God bless you and meet you at the very point of your need.

You can also send me an email to hello@madueke.com if you encounter any difficulty while writing your review.

PRAYER M. MADUEKE'S BESTSELLING BOOKS

Click on any of the [Buy Now] buttons to view or purchase them on my website. If you're viewing from a printed version, please visit **madueke.com** and search for these books.

1.	Dictionary of Demons & Complete Deliverance	[Buy Now]
2.	Monitoring Spirits	[Buy Now]
3.	Praying with The Blood of Jesus	[Buy Now]
4.	The Power of Speaking in Tongues	[Buy Now]
5.	Speaking Things into Existence by Faith	[Buy Now]
6.	Discerning and Defeating the Ahab & Jezebel Spirit	[Buy Now]
7.	Defeating the Python Spirit	[Buy Now]
8.	35 Special Dangerous Decrees	[Buy Now]
9.	21/40 Nights of Decrees and Your Enemies Will Surrender	[Buy Now]

10. Command the Morning, Day and Night   [Buy Now]

11. Evil Summon   [Buy Now]

12. Overcoming & Destroying the Spirit of Rejection & Hatred   [Buy Now]

13. Queen of Heaven: Wife of Satan   [Buy Now]

14. The False Prophet   [Buy Now]

15. Dominion Over Sickness & Disease   [Buy Now]

16. The Battle Plan for Destroying Foundational Witchcraft   [Buy Now]

17. The Queen of the Coast   [Buy Now]

18. Dictionary of Unmerited Favor   [Buy Now]

19. Prayers for Breakthrough in your Business   [Buy Now]

20. A Jump From Evil Altar   [Buy Now]

21. 100 Days Prayers to Wake Up Your Lazarus   [Buy Now]

22. Breaking Evil Yokes   [Buy Now]

23. When Evil Altars are Multiplied [Buy Now]

24. The Battle Plan for Destroying Foundational Occultism [Buy Now]

25. Prayers for Protection [Buy Now]

26. Prayers for Academic Success [Buy Now]

27. Your Dream Directory [Buy Now]

28. Prayers for Financial Breakthrough [Buy Now]

29. Destiny and Star Hunters [Buy Now]

30. Prayers to Pray during Courtship [Buy Now]

31. 91 Days Decrees to Takeover the Year [Buy Now]

32. Alone with God [Buy Now]

33. Prayers against Satanic Oppression [Buy Now]

34. Foundations Exposed [Buy Now]

35. Prayers for Deliverance [Buy Now]

36. Prayers to Heal Broken Relationship [Buy Now]

37. Prayers for Good Health   [**Buy Now**]

38. Comprehensive Deliverance   [**Buy Now**]

39. Prayers for College and University
    Students   [**Buy Now**]

40. 40 Prayer Giants   [**Buy Now**]

41. Divine Protection & Immunity While
    Sleeping   [**Buy Now**]

42. Prayers for Fertility in your Marriage   [**Buy Now**]

43. More Kingdoms to Conquer   [**Buy Now**]

44. Confront and Conquer your Enemy   [**Buy Now**]

45. Prayers to Raise Godly Children   [**Buy Now**]

4 Free Ebooks

In order to say a 'Thank You' for purchasing *Breaking Evil Yokes*, I offer these books to you in appreciation. Click or type **madueke.com/free-gift** in your browser.

Video Bonus

I've created exclusive video content to complement the topics covered in the book. These videos provide deeper insights and discussions on the things discussed in this book, offering you a more immersive learning experience.

To access the video bonus for this course, simply click or type links.madueke.com/6BEY in your browser.

Message from the Author

I want to see you succeed, grow, and break free from negativity and obstacles. My hope is for you to thrive, unaffected by negative influences and challenging situations. Because of that, please permit me to introduce two courses that I believe passionately will help you:

1. To break the evil altars and powers of your father's house, The role of altars in the realm of existence is very key because altars are meeting places between the physical and the spiritual, between the visible and the invisible.

    Unless a man cuts off the evil flow from the power of his father's house, he will not fulfil his destiny. **Click here** to learn more about **my course** on how to tear down unholy altars and close the enemy's entryways into your life!

2. To help you seamlessly break iron-like problems, illness, delayed marriage, poverty, or any long-standing battle.

    Discover **the transformative power of Christian fasting and prayer**. Remember, Matthew 17:21 teaches us, *"But this kind of demon does not go out except by prayer and* *fasting."* Ready to overcome your struggles? <u>Click here</u> to learn more about this course.

Embrace the journey ahead with faith, for through prayer, fasting, and the dismantling of evil altars, you shall unlock the doors to spiritual liberation and divine breakthrough. May your path be illuminated by His grace as you walk towards a life free from bondage.

If you're seeing this from the physical copy, type the link: <u>madueke.com/courses</u> in your browser to view all the courses on my website.

Prayer Madueke
CHRISTIAN AUTHOR

Christian Counselling

We were created for a greater purpose than only survival and God wants us to live a full life.

If you need prayer or counselling, or if you have any other inquiries, please visit the counselling page on my website to know when I will be available for a phone call.

Click or type **links.madueke.com/counselling** in your browser.

Let's Connect on Youtube ▶

Join me on my YouTube channel, "Prayer M. Madueke," where I share powerful insights, guidance, and prayers for spiritual breakthroughs.

Subscribe today to unlock the secrets of the Kingdom and embrace an abundant life. Let's grow together!

Click or type links.madueke.com/youtube in your browser.

An Invitation to Become a Ministry Partner

I appreciate the support and inquiries I have received regarding collaboration with my ministry. Your prayers and dedication to the work of the Kingdom are highly valued.

You can also visit the donation page on my website if you would like to contribute or learn more about supporting my ministry: madueke.com/donate.

Thank you for your continued support and faithfulness in Christ Jesus.